The Fighting Bradfords

Northern Heroes of World War One

Harry Moses

To my grandchildren – Emma, Leanne and Steven

Front cover:
Roland, Thomas, George and James Bradford at Milbanke House, 1914.

Back cover:
1. Family group, 1914. Standing: James with family dog and Roland; Seated: Thomas, Mrs. Amy Bradford, Amy, George.
2. George Bradford at stroke (right) during a training session in a whaler, c. 1917.
3. Roland Bradford, c. 1915.
4. The Victoria Cross.

© Harry Moses, 2003

Published by County Durham Books, 2003

County Durham Books is the imprint of Durham County Council, Cultural Services Department

ISBN 1-897585-75-6

Printed by Bell & Bain Ltd., Glasgow

Contents

5 Forward by General Sir Peter de la Billiere

7 Chapter 1: Early Years

14 Chapter 2: Growing Up

22 Chapter 3: Military Service 1904–1914

28 Chapter 4: 1914

35 Chapter 5: 1915

47 Chapter 6: 1916

58 Chapter 7: Roland and The Somme

72 Chapter 8: 1917

106 Chapter 9: 1918

116 Chapter 10: The Post-War Years

120 Chapter 11: The Bradford Legacy

123 Acknowledgements

124 Bibliography

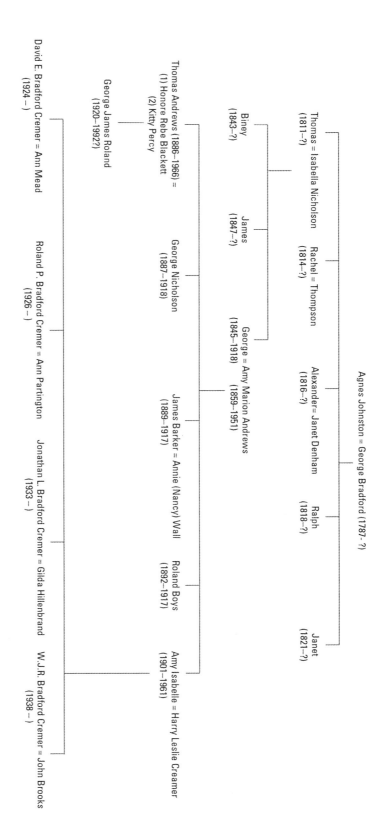

Agnes Johnston = George Bradford (1787- ?)

Thomas = Isabella Nicholson
(1811–?)

Rachel = Thompson
(1814–?)

Alexander= Janet Denham
(1816–?)

Ralph
(1818–?)

Janet
(1821–?)

Biney
(1843–?)

James
(1847–?)

George = Amy Marion Andrews
(1845–1918)   (1859–1951)

Thomas Andrews (1886–1966) =
(1) Honore Rebe Blackett
(2) Kitty Percy

George Nicholson
(1887–1918)

James Barker = Annie (Nancy) Wall
(1889–1917)

Roland Boys
(1892–1917)

Amy Isabelle = Harry Leslie Creamer
(1901–1961)

George James Roland
(1920–1992?)

Roland P. Bradford Cremer = Ann Partington
(1926 –)

Jonathan L. Bradford Cremer = Gilda Hillenbrand
(1933 –)

W.J.R. Bradford Cremer = John Brooks
(1938 –)

David E. Bradford Cremer = Ann Mead
(1924 –)

Foreword

General Sir Peter de la Billiere, KCB, KBE, DSO, MC*, DL

This book covers the lives of four gallant brothers, three of whom gave their lives in the bitter fighting of the First World War. In so doing they earned their country's highest awards for gallantry. One of the brothers, George Nicholson Bradford, who served in the Royal Navy, was killed at Zeebrugge on the 23rd April 1918, the day of his 31st birthday, and earned a posthumous Victoria Cross. Of the three remaining brothers, only Thomas Andrews Bradford, who went to France with the 8th Battalion The Durham Light Infantry, survived the war and was awarded the Distinguished Service Order. He was knighted for his services to the community in 1939. James Barker Bradford won the Military Cross in March 1917 for his leadership in carrying out an attack on a German strongpoint near Gommecourt on The Somme. He died of wounds in May 1917. He served with the 18th Battalion The Durham Light Infantry. The third brother to lose his life in France was Roland Boys Bradford who was killed on the Cambrai battlefield on the 30th November 1917. At the time of his death at the age of 25 years, he was the youngest Brigadier General in the British Army. This remarkable young officer had originally served with the 2nd, 7th and 9th Battalions of The Durham Light Infantry and was appointed to command the 186th Infantry Brigade, 62nd West Riding Infantry Division early in November 1917. Roland was a remarkable soldier, one who has been described as a genius by his seniors. He brought to command the essential skills of a fine tactical mind, complete confidence in his ability, rapid decision-making and outstanding courage. His men's needs were paramount and he held their complete trust. There is little doubt that, had he lived, he would have reached the highest ranks in the British Army.

I joined the 1st Battalion of The Durham Light Infantry in Korea in September 1952, as a young Second Lieutenant. This great Regiment is no longer part of the British Army but many of those serving at present in a variety of units come from the North East of England and particularly the County of Durham. North East men have a tradition of service for their country and many, like the Bradford Brothers, have died in that service. For me and I suspect for all who have served in that fine Regiment they have been icons of courage and as a family they epitomise the finest tradition of bravery and leadership within the British Services.

Chapter 1

Early Years

For many years on St. George's Day, the 23rd April, the following appeared in the memorial column of *The Times* newspaper:

> BRADFORD. In memory of Lt. Cdr. George Nicholson Bradford R.N., V.C. Zeebrugge, St. George's Day, his birthday, 1918, aged 31 and of Lt. James Barker Bradford, M.C., the D.L.I., France 1917 and Brig. Gen. Roland Boys Bradford, V.C., M.C., 2nd Bn. D.L.I., France Aged 25.

The memorial was placed in the paper by Mrs. Amy Bradford, mother of the four Bradford brothers who served in the First World War. Though filled with medals and honours, this brief tribute tells only a glimmer of the whole story. The Bradfords served with exceptional heroism in the Durham Light Infantry and Royal Navy, and George and Roland were the only two brothers receive the Victoria Cross in World War One. Three of them were to died in combat within a year of each other. As historian John Buchan said of the brothers, they 'found in a few years of campaigning a far richer career than most men who reach the full span of life'. Yet there was nothing in their backgrounds to suggest they might have become such warriors – they had a tough but middle-class upbringing in the coalfields of County Durham and no immediate military experience in the family. Not exceptionally gifted in school, to understand how these four rather unremarkable young men somehow found their calling in war, it is best to start at the beginning.

The name Bradford derives from the words "broad ford" – a crossing at a wide river. There is a Bradford village, near Bamburgh, Northumberland, that spans the Warren Burn, which flows through the village and reaches the sea at Budle Bay. The Bradfords of Co. Durham were originally a Border family who held land in this area. Little is known about these earliest of Bradfords, other than they were active during the turbulent days of the border incursions. There is a belief in the Bradfords of today that their forebears were Border Reivers, raiding and stealing in tit-for-tat clashes with their neighbours on both sides of the Scottish border, and that one member of the family was hanged for cattle stealing. At some point, the Bradfords lost their possessions in Northumberland and moved on.

The father of the four Bradford boys, George Bradford, was born on 21st March 1845 at Chirnside, seven miles west of Berwick-on-Tweed. Nothing is known of George's childhood, except that he was first educated in Northumberland where his family was involved in farming. He had two brothers:

George and Amy Bradford, December 1885.

Biney born in 1843 and James who was born in 1847. George completed his education at Houghton-le-Spring Grammar School in Co. Durham, and began his working life in the mines. Serving his apprenticeship in the Earl of Durham's Lambton Collieries, George eventually qualified as a mines engineer. His first appointment as a colliery manager was with Lambton Colleries. Later he was later appointed manager at Messrs. Stobart's Bishop Auckland Collieries, which brought about his ultimate move to Witton Park, three miles west of Bishop Auckland.

In the mid-nineteenth century, Witton Park was a small village in the midst of great change. The coming of the railways gave access to the South-West Durham coalfield, cheap coal and iron opened up the village to industrialisation, and workers flocked to the expanding opportunities. The 1841 census shows Witton Park as a few scattered houses, two collieries – Witton Park Colliery and Old Etherley Colliery – and the railway. In 1846 Bolckow and Vaughan began to build the ironworks, sited between the railway and the River Wear. By 1856, maps show a number of rows of back-to-back houses, brickworks, a railway station, a National School and two non-conformist chapels, one Methodist and the other Primitive. This same map reveals the home of the Bradford family, Carrwood Cottage (later called Carrwood House), in an isolated position on the main road into the village.

Witton Park continued to grow. By the end of the century, there were many more rows of back-to-back houses, separated by narrow alleyways in which large families crowded together. There was an increase in non-conformist chapels and a Church of England, as well as a number of public houses. Despite low pay and increasingly crowded conditions, there was little opportunity outside the village and the population became very insular. They had a reputation to be tough and hard working – many of them hard drinking – and though they might fight amongst themselves they provided a united front against any outside interference.

Into this small, compact and fiercely insular village, George Bradford arrived as manager of the Stobart collieries. The working men of the village expected in their bosses a strength and aggression that matched their own. George Bradford did not disappoint them. Strong-minded and physically tough, he stepped easily into the power his position gave him.

In 1885 at the age of 40, George Bradford married 26 year-old Amy Marion Andrews. Amy, born on the 29th March 1859, had lived with her parents and two younger sisters at Willesborough, near Ashford in Kent. Her grandson, George Bradford, son of Thomas, wrote of her in an unpublished autobiography:

> Kentish yeoman stock was her beginnings. A middling sort of background; perhaps if one scraped a little one would find clergymen, farmers and a lawyer or two. If there was not much money, there was certainly a compensating loving kindness and a confidence giving family unity…Their lives pottered along pleasantly enough until this uncouth northern intruder came along and changed everything…How did they meet? He, I think, had some temporary connections in the Kent coalfields, she had cousins in the north…meeting and proposal must have happened swiftly, marriage too, otherwise surely it could not have happened at all. They were an ill-matched pair. He, already over 40, uncouth and unyielding; she, her girlhood hardly over, inexperienced and sheltered. Trouble was inevitable once the preliminaries were over. From the first there was muddle and mismanagement from her, anger, sarcasm and complaining from him.
>
> 'She had a rotten life with him, poor thing', my father used to say.
>
> The surprising thing was that this unsuitable couple produced five remarkable and unlikely children.

Amy was a shy, yet attractive lady of gentle disposition. It was her misfortune to meet and marry a man who was almost her opposite in every way. George Bradford's personality and manners reflected his experience of a tough life amongst miners, and as he demanded obedience and efficiency in the running of his workplace, so he did in his home. He could be scathingly sarcastic, and it is possible that his bad temper and aggressiveness led to physical abuse. A wife with a stronger personality may have coped better with George, but Amy Bradford was not this type. Sheltered within her own affectionate family, she appeared to have had little training and experi-

Carrwood Cottage, Witton Park, now divided into two houses.

ence which would have enabled her to deal with the responsibilities she soon found thrust upon her.

After their marriage George Bradford brought his wife to Carrwood House, Witton Park, and an environment that was alien to her. From day one, Amy was expected to run an organised household, and she quickly had children to look after. Had she married a man of some patience and forbearance, she may have well learned to provide a home to her husband's liking. But her shortcomings caused friction, and it is doubtful that she gave sufficient guidance to the small household staff of two maids and a cook.

Amy was soon pregnant. The first of her sons was born on the 23rd March 1886. He was christened Thomas Andrews Bradford in St. Paul's Church

George and Thomas Bradford, c. 1889.

of England, almost directly opposite Carrwood House. The other three brothers followed in quick succession – George Nicholson on the 23rd April 1887, James Barker on the 11th December 1889 and Roland Boys on the 22nd February 1892, all of them christened in the same church. Sister Amy Isabelle was born in 1901 after the family had moved to Darlington.

Living in constant dread that her husband would discover her failures, her continual plea to her children throughout their young lives was, 'Don't tell your father'. This was probably made all the worse by the stress and fear of trying to please a husband who attacked her every effort. Not surprisingly, George was to assume charge of ensuring the four sons had adequate guidance and, especially, discipline.

The boys were reared in a tough regime laid down by their father. He believed that physical punishment moulded character, and that his sons should grow up to be self-disciplined, stable and independent. His grandson, George Bradford, wrote:

Their father would make his presence felt by a kick or a cuff whenever he came within reach of his sons. He believed that punishment should be administered on every possible occasion, on the assumption that even if it might not be merited at the time, it certainly would be before the day was out. This was the first principle of his views on education. Reading, writing and arithmetic were, of course, alright in their way but the rod must always come first. Nothing would be achieved in life, he maintained, without its frequent application to youthful bottoms.

It would be easy to condemn George Bradford for the harshness he exercised at home. In light of current child rearing practices, his methods are excessive, but the Victorian beliefs of his day differed considerably from those of today. 'Spare the rod and you spoil the child' was an attitude that was passed through generations, and one that was well cemented into George Bradford. Whether or not this was due to his own upbringing is not known, but it seems obvious that he grew up to believe that tough discipline had enabled him to succeed in life. It is possible that he had a latent affection for his sons that he found difficult to show. A photograph of George in old age with his arm around his daughter Amy suggests that he had mellowed,

James and his mother, September 1896.

and had a more open affection for her. Much younger than her brothers and the only daughter, she may well have been his favourite. Also possible is that George believed that expressing affection for his sons was being "soft", and he would tolerate no softness in his them.

If George had entirely had his own way throughout their young lives, there may have been little to admire in the boys' personalities. In their most impressionable years, a constant stream of corporal punishment and reinforcement of the belief that the harder you are the more success you will achieve in work, play and relationships, might have led to the boys' growing into adults with precious little feelings for and patience with others. As it was, they developed a tendency to see people as extremes – either good or evil. They had some difficulty in accepting that the personalities and responses of men and women fell between these two extremes, that people were, in fact, neither entirely good nor entirely bad. There is little evidence that they played with the local workers' children. Much of their free time seems to have been spent in the gardens of their homes playing amongst themselves or, as they got older, with the children of members of their own middle class. They were being groomed to lead and control working class men, not socialise with them.

Fortunately for the children, their father's life was an extremely busy one

Amy and her father in the garden of Milbanke House, winter 1907.

which involved a good deal of travel. He developed a small colliery of his own, thought to have been Caterthorne Colliery near Evenwood, and became chairman of the Newport Abercan Collieries in Wales. He was chairman of a steel company near Darlington and he also visited and inspected coal properties in Canada and Spain. Little evidence of any work in the community exists, though he was a school manager of the Local National School in Witton Park and his signature appears in the school logbook.

Sport was the one area in which George made a positive contribution to his sons' development, and he played a major part in encouraging them to take up boxing, cricket, soccer and rugby. If blows were meant to encourage toughness and independence, sport was an opportunity to practise and strengthen the virtues of courage, leadership and perseverance – plus the ability to take hard knocks without flinching and, if necessary, come back for more. When hurt it was vital not to show it but keep a stiff upper lip at all times. There was no place for tears in the Bradford household – certainly not while father was around. All the boys became proficient in sport and George (boxing) and Thomas (cricket and rugby) attained a high level of skill and success. In the classroom, learning took second place, as something to be endured before heading for the sports field.

Their maternal grandfather, George Andrews, also encouraged the love of sport. Over 70 years old when the boys were young, he had once been a bare fist fighter who had sparred with the well-known fighters of his day, Tom Sayers and Jem Mace. He instructed the boys in boxing, and was also a gifted storyteller. His tales always involved heroes who won through against all odds, which reinforced the boys' emerging senses of courage and duty. His visits were received with great excitement and the children clamoured for his time and attention.

As a balance to George's disciplinarian regime, Amy gave them the essential softness and affection missing in their relationships with their father. Her love, freely and equally given, did much to smooth the rough edges. It was to their mother that the children brought their cuts, bruises and tears, but only when father was not around. Her influence on her boys was considerable; a fact recognised in their letters of later years. Amy had a great love of literature and was instrumental in transferring the pleasures of reading to her children. Evenings before bedtime, the boys would gather around her chair in front of the fire. There, sitting at her feet, she read to them, and later they read to her.

Favourite authors included Dickens, Shakespeare, Stevenson and Longfellow. Heroic poetry was a particular favourite with the boys and they could recite 'How Horatius Won the Bridge' in full. Books on the history of the British Empire and regiments of the British Army aroused and strengthened their patriotism and pride in their country, and Wilson's Tales of the Borders reinforced their pride in their Border forebears. Heroic tales and poetry fired their imagination and many of the events described were enacted in the garden of their home. The choice of so much of their reading thoroughly imprinted on their minds the high ideals of leadership, courage, service and duty, which were to become so evident as they grew to adult-hood. One of the brothers, probably Thomas, wrote:

> I am sure that the reading aloud of all the best boys' books, in which the hero is such a gallant fellow and everything goes well with him had a most extraordinary effect on our characters. And this reading aloud by the family when we were at an impression-able age, stamped high ideals into us when we were children.

Later in life, their letters home instructed their young sister as to which books to read.

George is not mentioned as being involved in evening reading. Most likely, on his way to his club, he would open the door, snort his disapproval and leave. Paradoxically, their reading was reinforcing the very ideals their father was stamp-ing into them by more painful means.

Chapter 2

Growing Up

In 1894, the family moved to Morton Palms Farm, near Darlington. The healthy farm life further enhanced the boys' physical growth and fitness. The family lived here for the next four years, moving to Milbanke House, Milbank Road in Darlington itself in 1908.

Thomas and George probably commenced their education at the statutory age of five years at Witton Park National School. After the family moved to Morton Palms Farm, Thomas was enrolled in Queen Elizabeth's Grammar School, Darlington, on the 12th September 1894. George was enrolled at the same school on the 1st May 1895 (between these two dates he was probably at the Darlington Preparatory School). Both boys walked the eight-mile round trip to school, each day and in all weathers. No doubt this was part of father's 'toughening-up' regime. The brothers left the Grammar School in July 1896, and there is no record of the schools they may have attended until they were both enrolled at Eltham Nautical College. All of the boys seem to have attended a number of schools, moved around in their father's endless quest for discipline. Father believed that an efficient school was measured by the frequent use of the cane. Grandson George noted that such changes were usually announced at mealtime. At the end of the meal, George would look at the particular brother or brothers and announce that a new school would be started immediately where he could guarantee a more strict discipline and greater use of the cane than the one now attended. He would then stalk from the dining room leaving behind a silent and apprehensive family.

Thomas did not follow a career in the Royal Navy as his brother George was to do. The intellectual side of school life did not attract him and he put little effort into his schoolwork. On leaving college he went to live with an uncle who had a farm in Northumberland, where his love of country pursuits such as hunting, shooting and fishing had free reign. Finally he applied himself and qualified as a land agent. George continued his education at Eltham College. He had set himself on joining the Royal Navy, which he did as an officer cadet in 1902. He had worked hard in college and had passed the entrance examination for the Navy, listed as a modest 59th out of 77 candidates. His career in the Navy was to follow a steady if unspectacular rise through the officer ranks.

There are three schools on record that middle brother James attended: Bondgate Wesleyan School, Queen Elizabeth's Grammar School and Polam Grange School – all in Darlington. The only dates of attendance on record are for the Grammar School, which he attended from the June 1900 to December 1902. It appears that James was the least intellectual of the brothers and he is described in

Milbanke House, c. 1912. Now nos. 11 and13 in a terrace of houses, the Bradford residence can be identified by the crest above the bay window.

school reports as 'a plodder'. The following letter that he wrote at age 13 to his aunts, Mary and Bertha, shows an immaturity of style for someone his age. The sentences are very stilted and brief:

My dear Aunt Mary and Bertha. I hope you are getting on well. It is cold here. I have been sledging and tobogganing. I have got moved into the 2nd form. It is harder work. Baby [sister Amy] has got another tooth. We are reading a good book now. It is called *The King's Own Borderers* by James Grant. A school fellow of mine had his leg broken. A big boy pushed him of[f]. I have been up to see him. I took him a book to read. Tom is better now. We have some young hens. We get 4 to 5 eggs a day. We have knocked all the wall down. I have just finished my lessons. Baby can crawl now. I must be ending up now as it is bed time.

As James left Queen Elizabeth's Grammar School when he was 13, it seems that the lessons he refers to in his letter were possibly too difficult for him. His skills seemed to lean towards the more technical, and he went on to work for Hawthorn Leslie's Engineering Works at Newcastle and served his apprenticeship as an engineer. During this stage of his life, he lodged in Gateshead in the home of a Scottish widow and her two daughters. After qualifying as an engineer he returned to the family home at Milbanke. There is no evidence as to which engineering company he worked for but, at some point in time, he became a director of the Dinsdale Wire and Steel Company, near Darlington, which could have been the steel company of which his father was chairman. Except for the time spent in lodgings, it seems that James alone of all the brothers, remained at the family home with his mother and sister until he went to France in 1914. He was, also, possibly the most introverted of the Bradfords.

There is a great deal on record of Roland Boys, the youngest son. The unusual Christian name 'Boys' was derived from an ancestor of his mother's family, Dean John Boys (1571–1625), who was Dean of Canterbury Cathedral from 1619 until his death and was a noted theologian of his time. A Norman French name, 'Boys' was originally 'de Bosco', which developed into 'de Boys'. It has since

Thomas at Eltham Nautical College, and James in football gear outside Milbanke House.

been variously spelt 'Bois', 'Boise', 'Boyes' and ' Boyce'. It is believed that Roland's mother was descended from one of the Kentish family of 'Boys'.

Roland differed from his brothers in that he was mischievous, happy-go-lucky and full of fun, while the others tended to be sturdy and somewhat staid, attributes strongly developed throughout their early years at home. Sister Amy wrote:

> Roland was a tremendous tease, and he used to invent lurid crimes that my dolls had committed, and then he sentenced them to death and either had them hanged or chopped off their heads. He generally made up for the damage he had done, and once when he went to Darlington Fair he bought heaps of things and put them in my stocking. He carried 'Let's pretend' to any lengths. But although he was extraordinarily imaginative he could also be absolutely matter-of-fact.

Roland had a very alert and active mind, allied to a charm that often got him out of scrapes. It is possible that by the time he was born in 1892, his father's widening interests were taking him increasingly away from the family and he was seeing less of the children. Hence, his mother's lenient and affectionate response to the children may have had a greater impact on Roland than his father's influence. This in no way implies that father's influence was entirely lacking. He was at home on enough occasions to exert his authority, and Roland undoubtedly experienced his share of corporal punishment and his father's lessons on self-discipline, toughness and independence. In his relations with his father, Roland certainly challenged the rules far more than his elder brothers dared. His impish good nature often saved him if he overstepped the mark and, if he failed to do so, he took his punishment as his brothers did, fighting back the tears. He quickly got over punishment and bounced back in his usual buoyant and energetic manner. At school he was fond of practical jokes and, if any of these misfired, his charm often came to his rescue and saved him from reprimand.

Roland had a wide variety of interests, and flung himself wholeheartedly into learning to play the flute and mouth organ. Despite his enthusiasm he never achieved any great skill, unlike his older brother James and sister Amy who were the musicians of the family. The overall judgement of the family was that he wasn't much good at music, although he retained an interest in the subject throughout his short life. Another of his interests was cookery. He experimented with his own recipes for cakes and puddings. The results are not recorded, which may indicate that they were less than spectacular. Regardless of the outcomes, whatever Roland did, he did so with total enthusiasm for the time that it lasted.

From the earliest age, Roland was very much aware of his junior status in the family. He loathed being treated as the baby of the family, a status he held until the arrival of Amy when he was nine years old. He was very sensitive of his position and if anything truly upset him, it was being treated more like a child than his older brothers. Any suggestion that he was too young to have an opinion or to have his point of view heard in argument or discussion was met with forceful protestation. A limited edition book, *Brigadier General Roland Boys Bradford VC, MC and his Brothers*, was compiled and published exclusively for the Bradford family just after the end of World War One. Though there is no author identified with the book, it is quite probable that Thomas contributed extensively to it and may have written most of it himself. This family book contains many interesting and insightful anecdotes about the family and quotes Thomas's description of the young Roland:

> [Roland's] character was unusually complex, for it is no exaggeration to say that Roland, as a boy, was not always easy to understand. He was both exceptionally imaginative and casual, and he was also equally practical and matter of fact. When his imagination was enjoying one of its outbursts, it is quite easy to believe that he had astonished those who had, until then, seen only the practical side of his nature.
>
> I never saw him lose his temper, but he had a very quick tongue, and was very fond of argument. He disliked being suppressed on account of his youth, and would never quit an argument with his elders for this reason, and would stick to his opinion.

When Amy was born in 1901, Roland, though undoubtedly pleased to be relieved of the stigma of being the youngest, displayed a touch of resentment. He remarked that she would break up the balance in the games the boys played – invariably Roland and Thomas against George and James. However, he quickly realised that she would be far too young to take part, and his resentment, brief as it was, was replaced by a strong affection that his other brothers held – they loved their new sister wholeheartedly, and always referred to her by the pet name of 'Baby' and sometimes 'Ginger'.

Like his brothers Roland loved books, Dickens and Shakespeare being his favourites. He read poetry, committing much of it to memory to recite for members of the family or aloud to himself. Knowledge of books was not sufficient in itself; he craved vocabulary and composition, and as early as his teenage years, he decided that he must become fluent and articulate in speech. To attain this, he would shut himself away from the family and practice speaking aloud, usually long passages from Shakespeare and French poetry books. He carried this discipline into his army life, and would isolate himself in a tent or billet and practice speeches he had prepared, even down to coordinating the appropriate gestures in front of a mirror. His speeches to his troops reveal how successfully he had acquired this skill. One of his brothers wrote:

> Roland had far more brains than anyone of the family, and he was very vivacious, and we others were not.

At age 14, Roland kept a notebook entitled 'Scraps of Roland Bradford When a Schoolboy'. There followed a subtitle: 'My Pigeons, their Pedigree, and other things about them'. Very few of the entries have survived, but those that have indicate his developing skill for careful recording and an eye for detail, which came to fruition during his army career. He wrote:

> Flying Homers. The Huddersfield Pair. Cock,13 months. Hen, 15 months (June 3rd 1906). Bred. First egg, Jan. 20th 2nd Egg, Feb. 1st 1906. Both of them hatched but (Feb. 18th 1906) did not live, at least only one did (the cock). I think the cat got it. It was a great loss and a damper to me. Like a fool I omitted to ring them.

At the end of the year, he wrote:

> The following lines of Shakespeare are worthy of the hen. 'Age cannot wither her, nor custom stale her infinite variety.' Total at close of season, 8 eggs, 2 birds lived.

His notebook contained more than a record of pigeon rearing. Later entries included accounts of camps he had attended, a fictional thriller story and articles on keeping fit. Roland wrote several of the latter and some were published in Health and Strength magazine. Similar to his brothers Roland set out to achieve a high level of physical fitness, and would place a great deal of importance on physical training when he joined the army. Roland believed that if he could achieve fitness, so could others, and he was quick to offer advice. In one of his early articles entitled 'Neck Exercises' he wrote:

> The neck is part of the body which the Physical Culturists often overlook. It is quite common to see a well-developed body attached to a head by a thin, weedy neck. A bull neck is still more unsightly, but a neck obtained by physical exercise is shapely and handsome. As the neck gets very little freedom, being encased in a stiff collar during the day, I think it is of special importance that it should receive exercise.
>
> I give below the best exercises for producing a shapely and muscular Neck.

Another article advises:

> I would like to call attention to my readers to the value of 'Trunk Bending'. It assures a firm and graceful carriage of the body and embraces the whole system. A friend of mine, who had rather a large corporation, reduced his weight by a stone in one month by 'Trunk Bending'.

He even had advice for the ladies. Two articles in his notebook are titled 'Are Stays a Necessity?' and 'How to Maintain the Complexion'.

Roland was sent to Epsom College, Surrey, for his secondary education. Two letters that Roland wrote to his parents from here are still in existence. The first dated 9th December 1907 reads:

> Dear Mother,
>
> I hope you are quite well. I hope you will have a good journey. I went to tea with Mr. Lee yesterday. I am 9th in the form this term. I have just read the *Scarlet Pimpernel*; it is good. The sequel, *I Will Repay* I have been told is not so good. I have just had a letter from Father and Baby [sister Amy]. We lost our only match of the season on Saturday by one point against Charing Cross Hospital. Georgie is going home on the 14th I think. This is beastly ink. I hope the apples have been picked carefully in your absence. I think I will write to Firth tomorrow. You should pack in good time. I hope Grandmother is quite well. Tolley told me that Tommy had sent him a brace of grouse. I will take Baby some small present home, a clockwork doll or similar. This is the House notepaper. Are you going by the 10.35 from King's Cross or later in the afternoon. I go by the 10 or 10.35 a.m. Baby will be looking forward to seeing you.
>
> Thank you very much for the graphics which you sent recently – I did not acknowledge them in my last letter. I will not, like most schoolboys say, 'I must end up now because the bell is ringing for supper' but will bring the letter to a conclusion by sending my best love to all.
>
> Your affect. son,
>
> Roland

The second letter is dated the 16th June 1909, and shows his awareness of the fact that he had not achieved a very high position in his form. He offers the excuse of his age:

> My dear Father & Mother,
>
> I hope you are quite well. I am. Thank you for your letters. You will be receiving my half-term report. It will not be very good, I should say. My position in the form is 18th (out of 20). This is not so bad considering I am 8 months below the average age. Our school is placed above Rugby down at camp...
>
> We are mustering a contingent of 85 to send down to camp, besides Officers. I play for the Second XI. I saw Tommy's score in the Sportsman. It was very good.

The same letter shows despite his overall grades, his work in English composition continued:

> I was second in the English competition between the Classic Vth and the Modern Vth.

It consisted of writing a précis of Lord Roseberry's speech from memory in forty lines.

Roland attended Epsom College from 1907 to Christmas 1909, and did not complete his matriculation year. Like his brothers, his main interests were outside the classroom, being the sports field and the College Cadet Corps. He was a keen member of the Cadets, achieving the rank of Lance Corporal and Section Leader. He attended two Public Schools Camps at Aldershot in 1908 and 1909, referred to in his letter home. Roland's housemaster at Epsom, Mr. Lee, wrote:

> I remember him as bright, dark-eyed boy. He was never very prominent at work, and left us in the Matriculation Form. He was keen on fun and not above a practical joke, especially on the school sergeant at the store tent down at camp, but he was never a troublesome boy.

After leaving school at age 17 and with no qualifications, Roland showed an interest in medicine and, for a time, it seemed he was leaning towards the idea of becoming a doctor. He carried out a variety of experiments at home. Usually these took place in the breakfast room, where the lingering smells and remains of some of them were not well received by the rest of the family. Mostly, however, Roland went fishing and idled away his time to the point where his family were becoming concerned about his future. He joined the Church Lads Brigade at the Holy Trinity Church, Darlington, where the family worshipped and which was a short walk from their home. He soon became an officer in the brigade and attended the annual camp.

As they grew up, all the Bradford brothers took an interest in sport. Roland was particularly fond of rugby, and gained his first XV colours in his final year at Epsom College and captained his house team at half-back. His interest and involvement in sport continued into the army, not always without incident. Brig. Gen. H.H. Morant DSO wrote:

> In 1914, playing cricket for the regiment, he was keeping wicket to an unusually fast bowler on a hard, bumpy wicket. He missed taking a ball which never touched his hands but struck him directly on the temple and felled him instantly. The next moment he was up and ready to carry on with a bump as big as a turkey's egg already on his temple. I ordered him off, in spite of his vigorous protests, to have his head dressed. This gave me an indication of the innate and indomitable pluck for which he was famous afterwards.

The best cricketer was certainly Thomas. He played for Chester-le-Street in the Durham Senior League, and quickly earned a reputation as a stylish, hard-hitting, aggressive batsman. In a league game against Philadelphia in 1909 (referred to in Roland's letter home), he scored 207 runs in 90 minutes. He played for the Durham County Cricket Team between 1909 and 1914 and captained the side on occasions. He scored 1,519 runs for the County, which included four centuries. His highest score was against Cheshire in 1910, when he scored 168 runs. His final average for the County was 39.97. Thomas also played rugby for Durham as a forward, bringing the same enthusiasm and aggression that he showed at the batting crease. In 1911–12 he played against Cumberland and Northumberland, and in the following season against Yorkshire. He was also a squash player of considerable ability, participating in the amateur championships of the Squash Racquets Association. Thomas also hunted and was a keen fisherman.

George's great sporting skill lay in the boxing ring. The boxing lessons his grandfather had given him at home when he was growing up now bore fruit. He loved the sport and had the qualities demanded of the game – a high degree of fitness, skill and courage. An exceptionally fine amateur who won many prizes, George ultimately became welter-weight champion of the Royal Navy, and was reputed to be one of the finest boxers the Navy had ever produced. It was an interest of which his young sister was aware. In 1917 he wrote to her:

> Thank you for your letter and also the Hamlet that you are binding, it is just what I want…Yes I saw that Wilde beat Simmonds, I have seen the latter box, you are very observant to have noticed it.

George also played cricket and rugby, but had little opportunity for these, particularly while aboard ships with the Navy. Her wrote to his sister Amy on the 5th August 1917, from HMS Orion:

> It would be quite strange for Tommie to get busy with the cricket bat again. I have had two matches this year and performed indifferently well.

James was also a good local cricketer, and also played football, swam, boxed and wrestled. He had an affinity with animals, and his particular passion was horses. A naturally talented rider, he hunted with the Hurworth Hounds.

James and Amy, summer 1912.

Though none of the Bradford boys had an especially impressive academic record, their participation in sports and the discipline they received at home had formed them into physically fit, capable young men. Added to this was a belief in duty and courage that heroic literature and their grandfather's tales fostered. When war broke out in 1914, the Bradfords were exactly the sort of men who volunteered for their country.

Chapter 3

Military Service 1904–1914

Each of the four Bradford brothers chose to join the military in some capacity or other. Fit, active and interested in physical activity, voluntary involvement in the cadets and Territorials would have interested them. George was the first to choose the military as a career, using his training in the Eltham Nautical College as a springboard. From there, he attended Eastmans, which would prepare him to take the Royal Navy entry exam. He was accepted and proceeded to the Hindustan, anchored in the River Dart, and spent a few terms in training here before going to sea. The other three Bradfords joined the voluntary Territorial Forces; Roland took a regular commission in 1912 and Thomas and James were mobilised with their units at the outbreak of war in 1914.

On the 7th January 1904 George was appointed midshipman on the HMS Revenge. Two of his logbooks from this time, which cover the period of service from 7th January 1904 to 15th March 1907, are still in existence. Completed in his own hand, they give a record of his duties on the two warships. The maps and drawings in the books are meticulously produced and all entries are signed by his distinctive signature, 'G.N. Bradford'. George signed all of his letters, even to his family, in the same way. He referred to this habit in a letter to his sister dated 11th November 1917:

> Curious thing, I have never written George in my life – a quaint family in faith, pukha Dickens characters.

He moved to HMS Exmouth on the 18th April 1904, and was appointed Sub-Lieutenant on the 30th April 1907. On the 29th January 1908, he was transferred to the destroyer HMS Chelmer. It was while with this ship that he first showed his courage and total disregard for personal safety.

The HMS Chelmer, accompanied by the destroyer HMS Doon, was on its way to Dover pick up King George V and carry him to Calais on a state visit to France. At 3.30 a.m. on a very dark night, the 3rd March 1909, the Doon collided with a trawler 15 miles east of Owers Light. The destroyer's speed was 15 knots and its bow sliced into the port side of the slower moving trawler, which began to sink. Searchlights from the two destroyers lit up the stricken vessel, but the Chelmer's soon shorted out and could not be repaired. The rescue of the trawler's crew went ahead using the single searchlight on HMS Doon. The Chelmer launched its whaler, and Sub-Lieutenant George Bradford and a small crew rowed out to the stricken vessel, reaching it in about 15 minutes. George and his men rescued the three-man crew, and brought them back to the Chelmer.

During the rescue, no one realised that a boy member of the crew was missing. Due to a misunderstanding it was thought he had been rescued by HMS Doon. In fact, the boy had slipped while climbing the ladder to the upper deck, and had plunged down into the hold below and was knocked unconscious. Thinking that he was aboard the Doon, the Chelmer's captain began to pull away from the trawler, which was now about to slip under the waves. The Doon signalled that the boy was missing and was still onboard the trawler. In a desperate race against time, the Chelmer's whaler, still under the command of George Bradford, rowed back to the sinking trawler. Without hesitation, George jumped onto the trawler's deck and disappeared into the darkness, shortly to reappear carrying the unconscious boy on his back. He had no sooner got back into the whaler than the trawler sank. George's physical fitness and courage were brought to the attention of his superiors. As a reward for his brave act, he was promoted to full Lieutenant on the 30th July 1909.

George remained with the Chelmer until March 1910, when he was transferred to the newly commissioned warship HMS Vanguard. He remained with the Vanguard until the 24th January 1912, when he was appointed First Lieutenant on the HMS Amazon. He remained with this ship until he joined HMS Orion on its recommissioning on the 27th January 1914. HMS Orion was one of the battleships attached to the Second Battle Squadron of the Grand Fleet.

Unlike George, Thomas did not join the navy despite attending Eltham Nautical College. Instead, he returned to the North East of England and joined the 4th Volunteer Battalion, the Durham Light Infantry. He received a commission as a Second Lieutenant in 1906, and was promoted to First Lieutenant in October of the same year. In 1908, under the provisions of the Territorial Army Act, this battalion became the 8th Battalion Durham Light Infantry (Territorial Force), drawing its members from Durham City, Chester-le-Street and Houghton-le-Spring. Thomas was promoted to Captain in 1910, and ultimately commanded 'D' Company of the battalion, which drew its members from the Beamish area. Over the next four years until the outbreak of the First World War, Thomas attended weekly drill nights, occasional weekend camps and the annual camps. The commander of this group of volunteers was Lt. Col. W.C. Blackett, CBE, DL of Acorn Close, Sacriston, County Durham, who also owned a number of coalmines. Lt. Col. Blackett had a daughter, Honore Rebe Blackett, known as Rebe. Though there is no evidence to confirm it, Thomas probably met Rebe on several occasions, and may have begun a relationship that would culminate with their marriage in 1916.

In 1910, at the age of 18, Roland followed his elder brother Thomas into the Territorial Army. He joined the 5th Battalion Durham Light Infantry as a Second Lieutenant, and followed the usual territorial training calendar. His first annual camp was held at Richmond, North Yorkshire in the summer of 1910. At the annual camp at Featherstone Park, Haltwhistle, Northumberland in July of 1911, he received a telegram informing him that his father was critically ill and summoning him home.

Roland returned to Darlington at once to join his brothers. George was present on compassionate leave from his ship, and Thomas has travelled from his work as a land agent. James was living at home, and had been able to look after their father, mother, and young Amy, who was still only ten years old. There is no record of exactly what his illness was, but their father died within a very short time, at the age of 66. Following the funeral, Roland returned to complete his camp.

Roland Bradford, c. 1914

At the end of the 1911 camp, Roland attended a month's course at Colchester, based with the regular 2nd Battalion of the Regiment. This experience seems to have convinced him that his future lay with the regular army instead of the territorials. He joined the Special Reserve and enlisted the aid of a "crammer" in London to help him pass the entrance examination for a commission. He threw himself into an intense period of study and in March 1912, he passed the examination, placing 6th out of 36 candidates. In May 1912, he joined the 2nd Battalion Durham Light Infantry as a Second Lieutenant. His army career was fully launched.

On joining the battalion, Roland was 20 years of age, six feet tall, broad shouldered, athletic and intelligent, and full of enthusiasm. Capt. M. Jolley MC, who served under him when he commanded the 9th Battalion of the Regiment, wrote:

> The first time I met him, I was fascinated by his extremely piercing eyes, they seemed to bore right through me. He was very good looking, had rather an easy supple gait when walking and [was] very meticulous with his personal appearance and turn out, in fact, I used to think he was a trifle vain.

His boyish, mischievous personality had given way to a more mature and sober outlook and religion was beginning to play a vital part in his life. In the forthcoming war he was to view the Germans as the epitome of all that was evil and unholy, and he believed that God was on his side. Yet cruelty was not part of his nature, nor that of his brothers. Roland had no hatred of the Germans. It is possible that he thought by winning the war, the German people could be brought back to more godly ways. As we know, the Germans also thought that God was on their side.

He enjoyed talking with friends, and showed an interest in many subjects, especially but not wholly military. He studied the history of the Boer War and loved to discus the problems raised in this conflict. He would have found many others shared his interest: the Commanding Officer, Lt. Col. B.W.L. McMahon, was a veteran of the Boer War, as were some of the other officers. Roland also showed an interest in the social problems of his day, and was particularly moved by the state of the lower classes, especially women, who were badly paid and worked long hours in unhealthy conditions. His political leanings at the time might today have been described as left of centre. Capt. F.G. Maughan remembered Roland from the early months of his army career. He wrote:

> I was more closely associated with Bradford during the days of peace than in those times of war, for though I was in the same brigade with him after mobilization, I had ceased to command my company of which he was a subaltern.
>
> From the day that Bradford joined the battalion I was conscious of his strong personality and I think that others received the same impression. At the time we would not have expressed this in so many words, one did not stop to consider whether a newly joined subaltern was gifted with a personality or not, but merely formed a general opinion of whether he was the right material for making a useful soldier, whether he was likely to be a credit to the Army and his regiment. There were no two opinions about this as regards Bradford. From the beginning he was all keenness and enthusiasm in the right direction. He was ready to turn his hand to anything, no matter how unfamiliar the task might be and he would set to work with a calmness and often an originality of thought which brought success when older men did not expect that he would do more than make a good attempt.

He took a prominent part in all games, equally those with his men, organising and leading them but not interfering in the role of an officer in a manner to mar the men's enjoyment. Indeed both in and out of work, relations with his men were in accordance with the best traditions of the Old Army.

His activities were not confined to pursuits which appeal naturally to an athletic lad of 20. The spirit that prompted him to try his hand at everything and be defeated by nothing led him into unexpected channels. He occasionally wrote short stories, the theme generally being some incident in the hunting field. Though few saw these literary efforts it was generally known that they existed, and he came in for a good deal of chaff that, however, did not in the least damp his ardour.

Other instances of his minor activities might be quoted. He was in great demands at concerts at which he told amusing stories with much gravity. In some garrison churches it would become a custom for an officer to read the lessons. Bradford at once joined the ranks of those who were bold enough to undertake this duty, and as their numbers were few his willingness to do it was welcomed, and in addition, he read them very well. Performing at concerts and reading in church and much like things might have been regarded in many young subalterns as a desire to advertise and show off, which might have led to unhappy results but Bradford went about his way very quietly and with a peculiar dignity, which made it unnecessary to employ repressive measures in order to save him from wind in the head.

Roland drank and smoked very little. There was no sign of any young lady in his life and he seems to have shown very little interest in girls, so much so that his fellow officers, who charged him with being a 'woman hater', often pulled his leg. There is nothing to support this. In his home life he certainly loved his mother and sister with a deep and abiding affection. Roland, in typical fashion, threw himself into his new profession with complete enthusiasm and total involvement, which probably left little time for what he considered more frivolous liaisons with the opposite gender. The war, with all of its challenges and dangers, made opportunities for romantic contacts in his life even less possible.

The army challenged Roland's inventive mind and he quickly carried out experiments on a number of problems. He was concerned with how to protect soldiers while under fire. He experimented with an aluminium shield, light and easy to carry, that would give protection against enemy small arms fire. Tested on the firing range, it was found that the bullets went straight through the shield. His next invention was meant to deal with the problems that aircraft brought to the battlefield. At this time, aircraft were used mainly for observation, seeking out marching troops and directing artillery fire upon them. Roland came up with the idea of a fabric camouflage screen. On the approach of an enemy aircraft, troops could hoist the screen on stakes above the marching column. This invention did, at least, attract the attention of War Office experts led by Brig. Gen. Heath CB, who were given a demonstration at Colchester. The invention was not approved, but these failures did not cool his inventive fervour. Throughout his army career Roland continued to seek new methods of protecting his men, always trying to keep casualties as limited as possible. More and more his practices turned on the use of surprise and speed of movement, and an innovative use of firepower.

James in full Hussars uniform, c. 1913.

The last of the Bradfords into the

services was James. In 1913, he became a trooper in the Northumberland Hussars, a light cavalry brigade, and for an unknown time prior to that was a reservist in the Royal Navy. He appears in the Regimental Orders of the Hussars dated 4th July 1913, as No. 2187 Private J.B. Bradford, 'B' Squadron. This squadron drew its members from Darlington, Sunderland, South Shields and West Stanley and was commanded by Lt. C. Ferguson, with Sgt. Newstead as Troop Sergeant. As a member of the Hussars, James would have attended the annual camps at Blagdon, Northumberland in 1913 and at Otley in Yorkshire in 1914, and would have been able to continue his interest in horses. As war approached he became involved in recruiting friends and acquaintances into the unit. His sister Amy wrote:

> When the great recruiting time was on Jimmy got lots of recruits for the Yeomanry. Many of them had never been on a horse, and he used to teach them to ride and jump in the garden on Sundays, on his mare Kitty and my pony.

Despite James's willingness to encourage other recruits, there is some suggestion that he was a slightly less willing military man than his brothers. He joined the Hussars four years after even the youngest, Roland, had enlisted. Also, each of Bradfords attained the rank of senior officer in some capacity or other, but there is some evidence James would have been quite happy as a regular soldier. Given that he possibly had the least impressive school record and was probably the most introverted of his brothers, James may have been less confident about seeking the high level of appointment his brothers attained.

Chapter 9

1914

At the outbreak of war all four brothers were involved with the military in one capacity or another. George was a First Lieutenant on the HMS Orion; Roland was a Second Lieutenant with the 2nd Battalion Durham Light Infantry, Thomas and James were Territorials. Thomas was a Captain with the 8th Battalion Durham Light Infantry and James was a trooper with the Northumberland Hussars.

Unfortunately there are no official records as to George's duties on the HMS Orion. He does refer to his post in a letter to his mother dated 15th March 1914:

> Since I last wrote we have got through quite a lot of work and fired all the guns many times…I look after the boys (about 100) and I hope that they appreciate my genial, even temper. They are a very decent lot but need a good deal of 'chasing'.

There are also no official records to describe George's personal experiences during the war until the Zeebrugge Raid in 1918. The Orion was part of the Grand Fleet and the Second Battle Squadron during the war years, and by tracing their movements we can gain some insight into his wartime experiences prior to the raid.

The Grand Fleet was ordered to sea at 8.30 a.m. on the morning of the 4th August 1914, and later in the day the fleet received news that war had been declared. During the following three days the Orion and the rest of the fleet swept the northern area of the North Sea searching for German shipping. None being found, the fleet returned to Scapa Flow on the 7th August. Training, particularly in gunnery, followed during the next two days, and on the 9th August, the Orion reported a discovery. The crew had noticed a strong smell of oil and saw bubbles on the surface of the sea. This indicated the final resting place of the German submarine U 15, which had been rammed and sunk by the HMS Birmingham. The fleet also made periodic sweeps into the North Sea when sightings of enemy warships were reported, but few resulted in any contact. Between the 17th August and 9th September, the Orion was in Loch Ewe for engine repairs. It returned to the fleet to continue training and sweeps to the sea.

On the 16th December 1914, enemy warships bombarded Hartlepool, Scarborough and Whitby. The Second Battle Squadron tried to intercept the enemy ships on their return to Germany. Although the British warships got to within five miles of the enemy, they were unable to make contact, largely due to heavy mist. These events were the exception, not the norm, of daily life on board, and the early months of the war passed with very little excitement for George and the crew of the Orion.

Roland certainly could not complain of boredom and lack of action in the first five months of the war. In late July 1914, the 2nd Battalion was at an annual camp at Llanidloes, in Powys, Wales. They received the order to mobilise at 5 p.m. on the 4th August, and the battalion was rushed to Litchfield, Hampshire where it joined the rest of 18 Brigade of the 6th Infantry Division. Here the battalion was brought up to strength with an influx of 384 reservists.

On August 7th, the battalion left for Dunfirmline, Scotland where its brigade and division were concentrating. On the 13th August, it left for Cambridge and was encamped on Jesus Common with the rest of the brigade. From the 13th August to the 7th September, intensive training took place in the area. Roland was commanding a platoon in 'D' Company and was already gaining a reputation as an officer who demanded a high standard of training and fitness from his men. This reputation was already known in the family. His brother George wrote to their mother on the 15th March:

> Tommy told me that Roland's leave was curtailed on account of his Colonel wanting to start company training earlier. In fact, 'a Roland holiday cut short to butcher a company'.

On the 7th September, Roland and his battalion marched from Cambridge to Newmarket where they entrained late that night for Southampton. From Southampton they sailed for St. Nazaire, which they reached on the 9th. From there, the battalion entrained again for a long and weary journey to Coulommiers, east of Paris. After a short stay in St. Germain, on 15th September they marched 25 miles to Chateau Thiery, which was reached at midnight. Over the next few days march route took the battalion through Tigny, Chacrise and Bourg. Eventually it reached Troyon and went immediately into the front line trenches. A total of 80 miles had been covered on foot since leaving St. Germain. On the 25th September, Roland was promoted to Lieutenant.

The 6th Division arrived in France at the end of a long fighting retreat by the BEF and the French armies. Following the Battle of the Marne the Allies had pushed the Germans back and across the River Aisne. The British established their line on the front at Soisons-Bourg. The 6th Division joined I Corps of the BEF in the Bourg area. The Corps was extremely tired and weakened after the long retreat from Mons and the subsequent hard fighting on the Marne and the Aisne. Immediately on its arrival at the front, 18 Brigade relieved the 2nd Infantry Brigade of the 1st Infantry Division on the ridge north of Troyon, which was on the right of the British line. All companies of the 2nd Battalion were in the line. At dawn on the 20th September, the Germans launched a fierce attack and drove a wedge between the British 18 Brigade and the French Moroccan troops on the right. In the bitter fighting which followed the enemy occupied the trenches on the right of the Durhams.

During this struggle, 'D' Company commanded by Maj. Robb, which included Roland Bradford as one of its platoon commanders, twice counter-attacked without support and, it seems, without orders to do so. The enemy was driven off by mid-afternoon, but the Company suffered heavy losses. Maj. Robb was killed, and Roland was the only officer to survive unscathed. 'D' Company's total losses were 5 officers and 36 other ranks killed and 6 officers and 92 other ranks wounded.

A situation of stalemate now developed on the River Aisne. Both sides dug in and the notorious trench systems of World War I began to take shape. There was, however, still an open flank that stretched northwest to the North Sea, and with it a possibility of a quick victory if the Allied troops could outflank their opponents. So began what came to be known as 'the race to the sea,' as both sides tried to outflank the other. But as both adversaries tended to reach the open flank about the same time, the trench systems extended and manoeuvrability was lost. The BEF, seeking to safeguard the vital Channel ports through which its reinforcements and supplies moved, received the agreement of Gen. Joffre, commanding the French Armies, to move to the French left flank.

On the 25th September 6 Brigade was relieved, and Roland's 2nd Battalion marched to Peargnon. On route, Roland was promoted to Lieutenant. On the following day the battalion reached Vendresse, and on the 2nd October was holding a defensive line in the area of Ciry. On the 7th, it rejoined 6 Brigade and marched to Largny. By the 9th, it had reached Le Meux where it entrained for the move westward. During this march to le Meux an incident occurred that was witnessed and recalled by Capt. Birt, Roland's company commander:

> Roland and I were in the closest contact for seven bad weeks and I never saw him 'down' a bit, except somewhere near Compiegne. We had been marching all night and at about 6 a.m., came upon poor wretched refugees, old men, women of all ages on their way to Paris, with all their belongings on prams or in bundles. Roland was marching in the rear of the platoon and suddenly he came up to me and said, 'Do you mind if I fall out for a few minutes?' On my liberating him, he asked me for the spare bully beef and all the money I had (about 2frs. 85), and he fell out, to rejoin about a quarter of an hour later, hot from his run and evidently cut up. After tramping at my horse's side for a few minutes, he asked, 'Did you see that last lot of refugees before I fell out?…There was a woman among them who reminded me of my mother.'

Devoted to his mother, the plight of this old lady had moved Roland considerably.

On the 10th October, the 2nd Battalion detrained at Arques and went into billets. On the following day, it marched to Wardrecques and from there moved to Hazebrouck by French trucks. The plan was for the 6th Division to attack the line at Vieux Berquin-Merris, five miles east of Hazebrouck. By following the actions involving the battalion, we can obtain some picture of Roland's experiences.

On the morning of the 13th October the 2nd Battalion left Hazebrouck and marched to Vieux Berquin, which it reached at 2 p.m.. An advance guard of the 6th Division found the Germans entrenched on the east side of a small stream called the Meterenbecque. The enemy positions were very secure, situated on a long ridge near the small village of Meteren. Rather than engage the enemy in such an advantageous position, the battalion advanced to Le Verrière and was billeted in the Rue du Leet.

The 6th Division was now given the task of securing the bridges over the River Lys at Sailly. The 2nd Battalion marched overnight to reach Sailly, which although it had been set on fire, was clear of the enemy. The bridge across the river had been partially damaged but repairs carried out by the Royal Engineers enabled 18 Brigade to cross the river and take up positions south of the town. On the 17th October, the battalion was in the line between Tourquet and Le Quesne, just outside Bois Grenier. It was ordered to make a probing attack with a view to ascertaining the enemy strength at La Vallée. During the attack Ennetières was taken, and after this the 2nd Battalion went into reserve. On the 20th October the Germans counter-attacked against the British line, and the 2nd Battalion were recalled. At about 8.30 a.m. 'B' Company (under Capt. Wood) and 'D' Company (Capt. Birt) with Roland Bradford commanding a platoon, were sent to support the 1st Battalion East Yorkshire Regiment at Paradis. At 11a.m., Capt. Taylor's 'A' Company joined them. Severe fighting ensued with heavy casualties to both sides. The fighting continued over the next few days, and by the end of October only a handful of officers who had come out to France with the 2nd Battalion remained. Roland Bradford was one of them.

During this fighting, Roland was Mentioned In Despatches 'for gallant and distinguished services in the field' (*London Gazette*, 17th February, 1915). The following day, the Gazette reported that he has been awarded the Military Cross 'for services rendered in connection with operations in the field'. The outstanding part of 'services rendered' during this period happened on the 28th October when a particularly heaving enemy artillery bombardment fell on the battalion's positions. Roland's platoon was manning a barricade on the road between Rue du Bois and Wez Mocquart. Making use of the cover provided by ruined cottages, the enemy troops began to outflank and encircle the barricade. This possibility had occurred to Roland. He ordered a NCO and three men to take position on the Lille road and report on any enemy movement that would have threatened his position. It was Roland's intention to hold the barricade till the last possible moment. This he did. The same unnamed NCO wrote the following:

> We had another big do at Bois Grenier, and Lieut. R.B. Bradford proved at this period one of the finest officers I have ever had the pleasure of being with. We fought continually for two days and nights, but on the third night we were almost surrounded, and he gave me orders to watch the main road to Lille with three men; and when I gave my report to him he brought us out, and it was owing to his skill and valour that we got safely through.

The battalion was relived on the 21st October, having suffered heavy casualties, particularly in officers. The predicament in which Lt. John Harter described the battalion found itself in a letter to the Colonel of the Regimental Depot dated 31st October 1914:

> All moving about is done at night as by day shells buz in all directions. [Maj.] Blake has been killed, [Capt.] Northey is at base severely wounded. [Capt.] Wood was hit in the thigh the day I got here by one of his own sentries who had the jumps and his is very bad I'm afraid to say. Sisettinham Storey was killed by shrapnel. [Lt.] Park was looking for a site for his machine gun when he was killed by a random bullet, in the neck. Everyone speaks highly of him. Colonel McMahon is naturally rather worn out and worried at seeing all his officers go down, but those who remain are very cheerful…Sowers, Turner, Taylor, Bradford, Neil and myself are the only Regular officers here…We only have 18 of the original men left as the Company was decimated on the way here, and are now reforming with new men.

Just after this letter was written the battalion marched to l'Armée and into divisional reserve. On the 3rd November it moved to Chapelle D'Armentières and to Rue Delettre. It remained here until the 14th when it moved into the front line to relieve the 1st Battalion Shropshire Light Infantry at the Rue du Bois. In some places at Rue du Bois the trenches were a mere 25 yards apart. The battalion remained in the line until the 27th November. Roland's cheerful letter to his mother on the 21st made no mention of the ordeal he and his men had been going through:

> My dear Mother,
>
> Thanks for your letter and enclosure from Baby [sister Amy]. There is never any harm in mentioning places etc. in your letters. It appears that Jimmy's Regiment has been fighting on the allies' left wing. I am sending Baby a German helmet today. We are in trenches still. The weather is getting very cold but we wrap our feet in sacks and blankets at night so we do not suffer any discomfiture. The people at home are sending the men a large amount of clothing and tobacco etc., and I don't suppose they have been better off in their lives. I was very sorry to hear that Uncle Harold had been a little indisposed and I hope he is quite normal now. I hope you are enjoying yourself. I knew the Clayhills who has been killed in action. He was a nice fellow.
>
> Best Love,
>
> Your affect. son
>
> Roland B. Bradford.

After its ordeal at Rue du Bois, the battalion went back into reserve at L'Armée. The break was only brief, as on the 1st December the battalion moved to the front line trenches southeast of Chapelle D'Armentières. The weather was cold and wet, and remained so until the end of the year. During this period Roland and his men were in and out of the line or acting as reserve in the Pont de Nieppe-Armentières area.

Roland was the first Bradford to go to France, but James soon followed. James was serving as a trooper with the Northumberland Hussars as part of 'B' Squadron. At the outbreak of war, 'B' Squadron was training at Castle Eden in

County Durham. The squadron quickly joined the rest of the regiment at Gosforth and then moved to Lyndhurst in Hampshire in mid-September, to become mounted troops with the 7th Infantry Division. This division was earmarked to assist in the defence of Antwerp, which was being threatened by the advancing Germans. On the 5th October 1914, the division left Southampton for Zeebrugge on the SS Minneapolis, arriving on the 6th October.

No records of the Northumberland Hussars have come to light that mention James by name; after all, he was only a humble trooper. A Christmas card dated the 19th December 1914 confirms James' presence in France. It bears the regimental crest of the Hussars and is signed by James, with the additional remark 'to all at Dunns Hill House, thanking you for all the nice things you sent me'. It is only through the movements of the 7th Division and the role of the Hussars that we can put together a picture of what happened to James in France.

On landing at Zeebrugge, the Hussars moved to Bruges where they were enthusiastically received by the civilian population. They were billeted on the town football ground. On the 8th October, they went to protect the landing of the 3rd Cavalry Brigade, and spent the night in barns on the dunes near Ostend. The following day, they marched to Ostend and shortly thereafter entrained for Ghent. The first encounter with the enemy, which involved a Hussars patrol under the command of Lt. Joicey, occurred on the 10th October, when two horses were lost in a German ambush. We do not know whether or not James was a member of this patrol. Throughout the ensuing days, the Hussars acquitted themselves well enough to be accorded the following entry in the 7th Division History: '....the Northumberland Hussars did excellent work, showing considerable enterprise and initiative'. The retreat continued through Belgium and the division reached Ypres on the 14th October, joining the rest of the BEF, which was in the process of arriving from the east.

The First Battle of Ypres, which ultimately established the infamous 'Salient', commenced as the troops arrived and the Germans clashed with the hastily organised defence line set up by the Allies. The 7th Division fought in some of the fiercest engagements of this battle, at places whose names became synonymous with the courage and sacrifice of thousands of young men of both sides: Menin, Hooge, Polygon Wood, Zillebeke, Gheluvelte and others. The Hussars' role was to patrol and search for enemy units and to defend junctions between brigades and divisions – always weak spots in a defence line and sought out by enemy probes. On the 19th October, as part of an attack towards Menin, the Hussars were positioned at the junction of the 22nd Brigade and the 3rd Cavalry Division. On the 22nd, they moved to Hooge Chateau and, later in the day, to Klein–Zillebeke, always under heavy enemy artillery fire and fighting all the way. At Polygon Wood on the 24th October, the Hussars dismounted and, in an infantry role, attacked the German forces that had penetrated the wood. A battalion of the Warwickshire Regiment had been rushed up from reserve to meet this threat, and together they pushed the enemy back.

The crisis stage in the First Battle of Ypres commenced on the 29th October and lasted for the following six days. In the severe fighting over this period, the 7th Division was in the line at Gheluvelte–Zandvoorde. At the end of the First Battle of Ypres, both sides had fought themselves to a standstill and were exhausted. The conditions had been appalling and the losses extremely heavy. Recuperation and rest followed for the Hussars, and, throughout the winter of 1914, little of note took place. James Bradford had truly received his baptism of fire.

Thomas was the last of the three brothers to move to France. On the outbreak of the war on the 4th August 1914, he was with 8th Battalion, mobilised as part of the Durham Brigade of the Northumbrian Infantry Division (later 151 Brigade, 50th Northumbrian Division). Thomas commanded 'D' Company, with its headquarters at Birtley, near Chester-le Street. On day after war was declared, the battalion entrained at Durham station for the Monkwearmouth area to take up coastal defence. It manned the coast from the pier north of the River Wear at Roker to Whitburn Gas Works. Thomas's company held the area from Seaside Lane to the Gas Works, and spent the time digging and manning trenches. On the 9th August, the battalion was relieved and moved to the Cleadon and West Boldon area. On the 16th August, it marched to Gateshead and was accommodated in local schools and halls. Three days later it moved to Ravensworth Castle and into a large tented camp in the Castle's grounds. Here it remained for nearly 10 weeks, undertaking training and fitness exercises, and practicing weaponry and manoeuvres on the moors above Lanchester. Thomas threw himself into these physical activities with great gusto. He drove his men to reach, for many of them, new peaks of physical fitness. On the 2nd November, the battalion moved to the Sunderland Road Schools in Gateshead, undertaking guard duties on key points such at the Tyne Bridge and Newcastle Railway Station and Goods Yards. It remained here until the move to France in April 1915. Though Thomas's start to the war was slow by comparison to his brothers', it would not remain uneventful.

Chapter 5

1915

As the first months of the war had been unremarkable for the British fleet, 1915 was to prove a frustrating year for George Bradford. The Navy was eagerly anticipating action against their enemy. Would the German High Seas Fleet come out of its ports and confront the British? The British public awaited news that its mighty ships, which had controlled the high seas for so many years and protected the empire, had added to its laurels by defeating the German fleet. It was a disappointing year. The only real sea battle of note, the Dogger Bank action on the 23rd January 1915, was fought by cruisers and support craft on both sides. The Second Battle Squadron arrived at the scene to find that the enemy had again disappeared. King George V visited the fleet as it lay at Scapa Flow on the 17th July, providing an event to relieve the daily monotony. George's letters home did not show his disappointment at the lack of action and the boredom brought on by repetitive daily duties. He wrote to his sister in his usual light-hearted manner:

> Thank you for your letter. I believe you are the best writer in the family. I used to think that some girl wrote your letters for you. How goes the Algebra and the petite femme diable who teaches it? Glad the Zepps did not manage to pick off Pitt House. I should have thought Roland was just the man to come down to Wycombe and see you and put Mr. Whitbread right. I hope you did well at Lacrosse and also correct the 'gammie leg'.

Between short notes scribbled in a moment of leisure to his sister, George passed the year in a welter of training exercises, occasional sweeps to sea and submarine scares.

For his brothers, however, 1915 was to be a very active year. Following the fighting at Ypres, James's next major action was at the Battle of Neuve Chapelle in March. An incredibly bloody affair, the Hussars were reduced to 250 fit men by the end of it, and they assembled at Nouveau Monde under Maj. Backhouse. On the 15th April, James' 'B' Squadron was ordered to join the 1st Infantry Division at Locon and it remained with this division through the summer of 1915.

James had no ambition to become an officer. He was content and quite happy as he was, serving in the ranks with not too much responsibility. There is little doubt that he would have remained an ordinary soldier if it had not been for the pressure exerted upon him by his brothers to seek a commission. George, Thomas and Roland had joined their respective arms of the services as officers, and family pride demanded that their only remaining brother should become an officer also. Eventually, James gave way somewhat reluctantly. On the 18th September 1915, he was commissioned as a Temporary Second Lieutenant in the 18th (Service)

James Bradford, c. 1916.

Battalion Durham Light Infantry – also known as 'The Durham Pals'. It is a further indication of James' lack of ambition that he never advanced above the rank of Temporary Second Lieutenant.

It is difficult to discover the whereabouts of James during the first few months of his service with the 18th Battalion. There is no documentary evidence that James was with the battalion when it sailed for Egypt in December 1915. None of the family letters refer to him as being abroad and, unfortunately, no letters from James covering this period have come to light. When the battalion was raised in September 1914 the rush to join was such that it quickly grew to six companies. In May 1915, 'E' and 'F' Companies joined the second line of the York and Durham Brigade, which was retained in England. When James obtained his commission with the battalion, it is possible that there were no vacancies in the four first-line companies. He had experienced some hard fighting in the sanguinary battles of First Ypres and Neuve Chapelle; he had also spent his time as a trooper in the Hussars and had no experience of the duties and responsibilities of an infantry officer. It is quite feasible that for these reasons he was retained in England when the first line battalion went to Egypt. This would give him the opportunity to rest and learn these duties with one of the second-line companies. Whatever the reason, it has to be assumed that James stayed behind in England when the 18th Battalion sailed for Egypt.

Roland began 1915 with five months in the trenches. On the 1st January 1915, his 2nd Battalion was relieved and moved to Houplines. Until early May, when Roland would leave the battalion, it spent time between the front line trenches in the Houplines area and at rest in Armentières. Considered a 'quiet' area, each day started and ended with artillery bombardment from both sides, which came to be known as the morning and evening 'hate'. In keeping with the general policy of the British army, the battalion sought to dominate no man's land through active patrolling. German snipers, though, were also very active. Casualties were a daily occurrence, and the losses were replaced by periodical drafts of officers and men from England. The weather didn't help; the winter of 1914–15 was cold and wet, with heavy snowfalls. Trenches had to be continually repaired and this work could only take place at night. In February, the battalion received warm winter clothing from County Durham through the efforts of the Lady Londonderry organisation. This included warm underclothing, mitts and socks. As a bright patch in a dreary season, on the 3rd March 1915, Roland was promoted to Temporary Captain.

Meanwhile, on Monday 19th April 1915, Thomas left for France with his 'D' Company and the rest of the 8th Battalion. They marched through the streets of Newcastle to the Central Station where dense crowds of well-wishers and relatives had gathered to give them an enthusiastic send-off. The regimental band played, civic dignitaries shook hands with the commanding officers and the troop train pulled out of the station to loud cheers and not a few tears. The battalion detrained at Folkestone and left on the same evening for Boulogne, arriving at 1 a.m. on the following morning. It marched up the steep hill to St. Martin's Camp, Ostrovhe, which was tented and overcrowded. Awakened at 8 a.m., they had breakfast and paraded for the march to the railway station at Pont des Briques on the southern outskirts of Boulogne. Here they entrained for Cassel, the officers in draughty carriages and the men in trucks marked '8 chevaux ou 40 hommes'. Cassel was not reached until 7 p.m. on the 20th April. From the station a further march followed to the village of St. Marie Cappelle, which was reached about midnight. The men were billeted in barns, the officers in farms and houses in the village. Thomas and his fellow officers found themselves censoring the men's letters for the first time and dealt with the contents with meticulous care and discretion. For a few days, the officers and men enjoyed a relatively relaxed yet busy period as the division checked kit, equipment, weapons and stores prior to commencing training.

Usually, when a newly arrived and inexperienced division entered the war zone, the new soldiers were gradually integrated into the fighting line. They would have the opportunity to learn from more experienced units over several weeks until they were confident in their abilities in the front line. The German gas attack on the 22nd April in the northeast sector of the Ypres Salient put an end to such plans. The gas opened a huge gap in the Allied lines for the advancing enemy infantry. Units were flung into battle as an attempt to seal the gaps as and when they occurred. Junior officers and men fought where they stood and died to prevent a German breakthrough. The Northumbrian Division was to be thrown into this battle a mere three days after its arrival in France. The Second Battle of Ypres was underway, and Thomas Bradford was on his way to join it.

On 23rd April, a Friday morning while the 8th Battalion was still billeted in St. Marie Cappelle, orders came to be ready to move at short notice. At 1.45 p.m. the battalion formed up on the road through the village and marched to Riveld where it joined the remainder of the Durham Brigade. The brigade then marched to Steenvoorde. It was here that the officers and men first realised that something serious had occurred. Both French and British troops were rushing up the road towards Ypres in motor transport and on foot. Thomas and his company, along with the rest of the battalion, were put onto London double-decker buses. They drove up the pavé road towards the French–Belgian frontier, crossing at Abeele and travelling on to Vlamertinghe, which they reached at 11 p.m. Sprits were high and the men sang and joked throughout the journey. At Vlamertinghe, billeted in the convent and its outbuildings, they waiting for the order to move forward. The realities of war were now clearly visible. Quite close to the billets was a Canadian hospital, which was flooded with the victims of gas and gunfire. The pitiful sights of wounded and gassed men, together with the noise of battle only a few miles ahead, sobered the initial enthusiasm.

During the 24th April, the battalion stood to with orders to prepare to move at a moment's notice. It was not called upon until 6.30 p.m. when the men were drawn up and marched off towards Ypres. It was a march that Thomas and his men would never forget. Never having a shot fired at them in anger, they marched towards the sound of the guns. A constant stream of ambulances carrying wounded and gassed men passed them in the opposite direction. Terror-stricken refugees pushed or carried their meagre possessions towards the rear. These sights of men, women and children driven from their homes, the innocent victims of war, were unforgettable. A fellow officer described that march and the battalion's first experience of enemy gunfire. Capt. Frank Harvey, commanding 'A' Company wrote:

Ypres was being heavily shelled, but there was no way round, so we had to march through. Ypres has left an impression on my mind. The dark houses silhouetted against the sky, some entirely wrecked, an occasional glimmer of light from a cellar, the deserted streets with here and there a dead civilian lying beside his bundle of goods, and dead horses and men. A shell screamed over us and burst with a deafening roar. We closed up a bit and quickened our pace. I think we were all glad to reach the open country beyond. Potijze lay a complete wreck across the road.

The battalion was placed under the command of Brig. Gen. Chapman, GOC 85 Brigade, 28th Division. Verlorenhoek, a short distance beyond Potijze, was reached at about 11 p.m. The battalion passed through the village and took up positions left and right of the road to Zonnebeke. Here the men sheltered in the hedgerows with orders not to move until told to do so and, if they were still in position at dawn, to avoid observation from the circling German aircraft. Rain started to fall upon the men who were already dead tired after their long march. Verey lights soared into the night sky all around them. Shells passed overhead and a farmhouse burned fiercely close by. Any opportunity to sleep ended in the middle of the night when they received orders to form up on the road and prepare to move. Thomas and his 'D' Company led the battalion, followed by 'A', 'B' and 'C' Companies, in that order. Progress was very slow. There were many stops in the darkness, and rain continued to drench the increasingly tiring men. In addition to their usual equipment and weapons the men carried extra ammunition and what was left of the day's food issue and their iron rations. This was not the glorious entry into battle they had imagined; more a shuffle into a dark and dangerous unknown. Capt. Harvey wrote:

> It was rather a weary march in the wet, as it was difficult to keep closed up and we had numerous short halts…We left the road and took a side path along the railway track and skirted Zonnebeke, which was in ruins, and closed up again on the road bearing to the left. We eventually reached a farm at the crossroads, occupied by Canadians. I asked a sentry how far it was to the trenches and was told that they were a couple of miles further on. We had a brief halt there and then led on again. It was not until there was a faint glimmering of dawn that I realised that the two rear companies had halted and that 'D' and 'A' were going to the trenches led by a Canadian guide. I could not understand why dead lay in all directions if the trenches were still so far ahead, and many appeared to be half-stripped of their clothing; the peculiar scent of chlorine in the air…

'D' Company followed by 'A' Company, left the rest of the battalion at Boetleer Farm. Thomas described the move into the front line:

> 'D' Company moved off with a Canadian guide. 'A' Company followed immediately behind. From Boetleer Farm we moved up slight rising ground then over gradually falling ground and turned left into a trench held by Canadians. The distance from the farm to the trench would be at least six hundred yards. 'D' Company moved along this for some two hundred yards, then came to what was a communication trench containing much water, and eventually some two hundred yards further on, reached a trench also held by Canadians, whom the company relieved. The left flank of this trench was turned to the rear at a right angle. A portion of the trench, about its centre, was a communication trench. The two companies were placed on each side of this. This line of trench had originally been French, there being dead buried in and around it; the bodies, which had only been buried in shallow ground, were thrown up by shell fire during the day, and were French Colonial troops. The trench was shallow with a good breastwork, but no parados. It contained a number of dug-outs, one occupied by Signals, the rest filled with dead, wounded and gassed Canadians, mostly the latter…

The Germans held trenches about 150–200 yards ahead. It was about 3 a.m. on the morning of Sunday 25th April 1915.

The two companies held a dangerous outpost position, isolated from the rest of the battalion, which was held back at Boetleer Farm. The position was threatened on three sides by superior numbers of German troops, supported by overwhelming firepower from guns of all calibres. It was a hopeless position, which the Canadians that they were relieving quickly pointed out to them. It was a situation that called upon all the aggression, enthusiasm, drive and leadership that Thomas had displayed so often on the playing fields and had been instilled into him for most of his life. His large, solid frame, conspicuous throughout the day as he moved amongst his men, was a source of strength to many. The situation was made much more desperate by the inexperience of officers and men as they faced an enemy whose strength and ruthlessness were most obvious. They faced their ordeal with an enthusiasm that only their ignorance of what was to come allowed them to have.

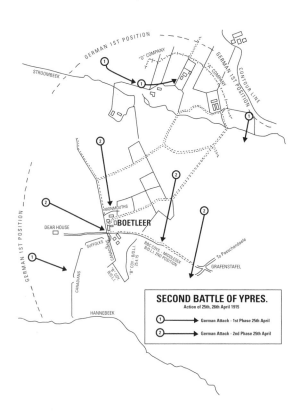

The Second Battle of Ypres, action on 25–26 April 1915.

At about 4 a.m. heavy enemy shelling fell on the farmhouse and the ridge behind them. Communications soon failed and the two isolated companies were unable to establish contact with battalion headquarters for the rest of the day. The morning was spent observing enemy troop movements in front of the companies' positions and towards the open flanks. About mid-morning, Thomas became concerned about German troop movements towards his open left flank and asked Capt. Harvey of 'A' Company to join him in observing the enemy activities. The two commanding officers discussed the situation. It was observed that many of the enemy were dressed in blue uniforms and not the expected field grey. Capt. McLeod, a Canadian officer who had stayed behind to assist the Durhams during the initial settling in, confirmed that the enemy were German Marines who were now working round 'D' Company's left flank at a distance of about 1,000 yards. The Durhams opened up rifle fire on the enemy and kept them at bay. Some Canadians had volunteered to stay behind and provide machine gun support for the two companies. Their profane disrespect for the Germans did much to raise the spirits of the green British troops. Neither of the two British companies had brought machine guns with them, though they had a number of gunners and belts of ammunition. Unfortunately, the ammunition was of no use as it was of a different calibre to that used in the Canadian guns.

A German observation plane flew constantly over the trenches and the Durhams vainly attempted to shoot it down with rifle fire. On one of its runs it dropped some glittering paper just above the companies' positions. The reason for this soon became clear as a few minutes later a heavy and sustained enemy bombardment fell upon the trenches. Shells were exploding around and on the breastworks and casualties mounted alarmingly. A number of Thomas's junior officers were wounded or killed within minutes, together with many of his men. There were no parados to protect them against shells that landed behind the breastworks and, at this early period of the war, there were no steel helmets to protect against head wounds. The scene was one of chaos and destruction, with the screams of the wounded merging with the ear-shattering noise of exploding shells that rained down upon them. The dwindling numbers of officers and NCOs tried to make themselves heard above the din. There was nothing the men could do but take this hell that broke over them, cowering in what little shelter the disintegrating breast-work could give. British artillery support was almost none-existent; all that they could do was to curse, cry and pray. The badly wounded tried to crawl to shelter in the few dugouts, which were already crowded with Canadian wounded. Soldiers tried to stem the flow of blood from ugly, gaping wounds with inadequate shell dressings. There were many instances of individual courageous acts as men risked their lives to pull wounded comrades to the safety of some shelter. A few men cowered against the breastwork, their nerves shattered, unable to control their shaking limbs or the tears streaming down their faces. Yet throughout this ordeal of fire, the majority of men responded to the commands of their officers and NCOs and manned the shattered breastworks to await the inevitable German infantry attack, which must follow.

This was the day, the very moment, when Thomas was to be truly tested as a leader of men. Whilst chaos reigned all about him, everything he did, every word he spoke, every command he gave, every movement of his face and eyes, was scrutinised by his men as they looked to him to hold them together. Had he shown weakness, fear or uncertainty, disaster would have been complete. He was every-where, rallying his men, encouraging, rapping out precise orders and showing a complete disregard for his own safety as he fought to bring order out of confusion. He rallied the survivors and when the German infantry attack came in, it was beat-en off. This unsuccessful attack was followed by another barrage of high explo-sive shells, mixed with shrapnel, from the enemy artillery as it sought to blast the company out of its position.

By early afternoon, Thomas was becoming increasingly concerned about his open left flank, which was coming under enfilade fire. Runners were sent to try and contact battalion headquarters in Boetleer Farm but, if they got through, no message of support was forthcoming. Thomas ordered Lt. Wilson to take a party of men and extend his left flank to meet the threat. Wilson and his men took up position in a field of mustard but were unable to dig in before the enemy machine guns located them and inflicted heavy losses on the party. Wilson was wounded and many of his men were killed. The Germans made another determined attempt and, yet again, were driven off by rapid rifle fire. These successes raised the spirits of the survivors of 'D' Company but they must have been quickly lowered by what happened next. Some two miles away, trains drew up on the Ypres–Standen railway, full of German infantry. These forces detrained, formed up and moved towards the Durhams' positions. The Germans attacked again with their vastly superior forces, but were driven off with great loss once more. As each attack was repelled the enemy saturated the company positions with artillery fire and many of those who had survived so far became casualties.

It was now late afternoon and the situation was becoming desperate. Thomas had lost most of his officers and NCOs. His company was down to nearly 30 fit men, out of an original total of about 200. The Germans were actively working round his open left flank. Both 'D' and 'A' Companies – the latter of which had also been under continuous enemy attack and suffered heavy casualties – had contracted their positions to make defence more manageable with the small number of men available. Ammunition was low. The men were desperately tired. The German guns continued their remorseless hammering of the already battered breastworks and casualties continued to increase. At about 5 p.m. another German attack was driven off but it was now clear that the Durhams would have to retire. The prospects of getting away were extremely thin. The only way out was through the fields to the rear, which sloped up to Boetleer Farm. These were completely devoid of any cover, and swept continually by enemy artillery and machine gun fire. Thomas and his men, along with those of 'A' Company, had done far more than could have been asked of them. They had marched most of the night, and fought and held the position all day. They had exacted heavy losses on the enemy but had suffered grievous casualties themselves. At 5.30 p.m. the only remaining machine gun ran out of ammunition. There was now very little to fight with other than bayonet and bare hands, and the numbers capable of fighting were pitifully small. No relief was imminent as, unknown to the companies, the remainder of the battalion at Boetleer Farm was under constant artillery and machine gun fire and infantry attack.

At about 6 p.m. Thomas gave the order to retire through 'A' Company's positions on their right. Capt. Harvey of 'A' Company wrote:

> Just after 6 p.m. we saw figures dodging along the sector we had vacated and the guns swung round. Fortunately a shout from one of our men stopped the fire. We recognised Captain Bradford and about a dozen of his men. He jumped in amongst us…I had a moment's conversation with Captain Bradford and then he passed through with his men.

'A' company retired about one hour later.

Thomas was the last to leave his position. He worked his way to the rear through shell and machine gun fire, searching for battalion headquarters. He lost his way and found himself with the 2nd Battalion Northumberland Fusiliers of the 28th Division. He had been wounded in the hand. Of the fine company he had commanded when he left England, about 200 strong when he led it into the breastworks early on the same morning, 7 officers and 173 other ranks had been killed, wounded or were missing. They were men he had commanded and come to know well, and he felt a deep sense of responsibility for their welfare and safety. He had left many of them amongst the shambles of the trenches. In very low spirits, he made his way to the rear. He reached Vlamertinghe on the following day and must have received medical attention for his wounded hand and stayed on duty. Here he was joined by a small number of 8th Battalion stragglers who came in over the next few hours. These numbers gradually increased. On the 3rd May, with 120 men he had gathered up, he rejoined the battalion at a rest camp near Brielen.

Capt. Northwood, an officer of the Canadian battalion relieved by 'D' and 'A' Companies, spoke to an officer of Thomas's company when both were in the same prison camp in Germany. He said:

> Such bearing would have been splendid even in a regiment of veterans. But to think, the majority of them were boys, and for the first time under fire. It was a shame to allow them to relieve part of our battalion.

We next hear of Thomas on the 13th May 1915. On this day, the 8th Battalion was sent to assist the cavalry who were heavily engaged in trenches to the east of Ypres. The companies were sent into dugouts near Potijze Chateau. One company, with Thomas in command, was placed south of the Ypres–Verlorenhoek road and was shelled all the way into the trenches they were to occupy. Fortunately, only two men were wounded during the move. While filing along a trench into position, a cavalry officer enquired, 'Who are you fellows?' On being told 'Durhams' he exclaimed, 'Thank God; now we'll get some good digging'. The Durham reputation for digging fast and deep, the lifetime skills of miners, was already well known amongst other regiments.

On the 13th and 14th May the battalion was heavily shelled. On the 15th, it was relieved and moved to Brielen. During the next few days the battalion dug trenches, often under enemy shellfire. On the 22nd, Thomas's company was in trenches at the northeast corner of Potijze Wood. On Whit Monday, 24th May, the Germans released a dense cloud of poison gas and launched a major attack on the British front line. At 12.10 a.m., the 8th Battalion was ordered to move to a level crossing on the Ypres–Roulers railway, close to Railway Wood. Thomas's company led this advance. It was hoped that the cover of a hedge would protect them from the German artillery observers, but this was not to be. A German balloon spotted them during the move and they came under heavy shellfire. They moved quickly into the trenches of the GHQ Line, where further movement proved to be very slow as these positions were already full of troops. On reaching the railway station, the battalion's way was blocked by thick wire entanglements across the line, which was also covered by enemy guns. Thomas, under enemy fire, crawled forward and cut a way through the obstruction. The men darted across the railway line in small parties of about six at a time and reached the cover of the railway embankment. Thomas led them along the railway line, suffering some casualties as they came under rifle fire from the German positions. The rest of the battalion followed closely behind. On reaching the crossing, they discovered that in order to relieve the 3rd Battalion Royal Fusiliers, they would have to cross some 200 yards of open ground. The relief was carried out with a surprisingly small number of casualties. The battalion held this position was until the following day when it was relieved.

Losses overall had been high and the battalions were reorganised. On the 8th June, the 6th and 8th Battalions were formed into a single composite battalion. 'A' Company of this battalion was made up of the survivors of the 8th Battalion and was commanded by Capt. Thomas Bradford. The other three companies of the composite battalion comprised 6th Battalion personnel. Time and again, Thomas and his company had been chosen to lead the battalion into the most difficult situations and this may well reflect upon his growing reputation as a fine company commander. Thomas's movements from this time are not well documented and it is only by tracing the movements of the battalion that we can obtain a somewhat sketchy picture of his activities.

In mid June 1915, the composite battalion was in the line in the Sanctuary Wood sector of the Ypres Salient. On the 24th June, it moved into the Neuve Église–Kemmel sectors and a quiet period ensued. In the second half of July, the battalion moved to Armentières where, on the 11th August, having received new drafts, the 6th and 8th Battalions reverted to their original and separate identities. The 8th Battalion, with Thomas as company Captain, remained in the Armentières area until mid November. It was a relatively quiet time with most activities confined to patrolling and searching for snipers. As the winter deepened, the Durhams devoted most of their time to repairing and improving trenches and seeking to improve living conditions. In mid December, the battalion was back in the line in the Sanctuary Wood sector. An enemy attack including poison gas and heavy shelling was launched on the 19th of the month, but was beaten off. Throughout December, the conditions in the trenches were terrible. Icy water and mud were everywhere, and Thomas and his men had an extremely uncomfortable time of it.

Life for the other Bradfords was not dissimilar, but a major high point came on the 3rd of May 1915, when Capt. Roland Boys Bradford was posted as Adjutant to the 7th Battalion Durham Light Infantry, a territorial battalion with the 50th Northumbrian Infantry Division. Roland had written to his mother on the 2nd May informing her of his promotion:

> I leave today to take over Adjutant of the 7th Battalion Durham Light Infantry Northumbrian Division, Expeditionary Force. (New address). I will probably not be able to write to you for some few days.

She must have been quite proud of his achievement. The position of Adjutant in a battalion was an important one, and one which any young officer could expect to hold at some time in his career. As the administrative officer of the battalion, the Adjutant job was to ensure the smooth daily running of the battalion, and draw up and issue the orders of the commanding officer. Organised and efficient,

Roland would have been well suited to his new role and he must have been looking forward to taking it up.

The 7th Battalion was a territorial battalion, raised in the Wearside area of Durham County. It moved to France in April 1915 with the Durham Brigade of the Northumbrian Division, renamed the 50th Northumbrian Infantry Division in May of 1915. The commanding officer was Lt. Col. E. Vaux of the well-known northern brewery family. He had already seen service during the Boer War with one of the volunteer service battalions. Within five days of arriving in France, the 7th Battalion along with the 6th, 8th and 9th Battalions of the regiment and, indeed with the rest of the division, was flung into action in the Ypres Salient during the crisis caused by the surprise German gas attack which commenced on the 22nd April. It had sustained heavy losses and amongst the casualties was Capt. R.B. Bergne, the battalion Adjutant whom Roland replaced. Unfortunately, there is little information available that describes Roland's personal experiences with the battalion, but we can get an idea from the War Diaries of the battalion.

As described, the various, newly arrived battalions of the Northumbrian Division were flung piecemeal into the caldron of Ypres, and were temporarily attached to other divisions and brigades who were fighting to hold the German onslaught. On the 3rd May, the 7th Battalion was resting in billets at Watou, which was where Roland joined the battalion.

On the 5th May, Gen. Sir John French, Commander-in-Chief of the BEF, spoke to the 7th and 9th Battalions Durham Light Infantry. Drawn up before the General, the survivors of the battalion's recent actions had their first good look at their new Adjutant. An unnamed eyewitness later wrote:

> The remnant of the 151st Brigade was drawn up for inspection by our Commander-in-Chief, then Sir John French. It was then that Capt. Bradford…stood in a striking silhouette to those who noticed him, alongside our Colonel. A pleasanter smile no man could have seen than on Capt. Bradford on that particular day, and he was among strangers of whom he could know nothing.
>
> Even in September 1917, when last I shook hands with him (prior to taking up his new command as Brigadier), he still had that old 1915 smile, but on a scarred face caused by a wound that had not healed.

There were those who thought that Roland's soldierly qualities would be wasted with a pioneer battalion, which the 7th soon became, and he would find his tasks tedious and unchallenging. He may have longed for a return to a front line battalion but it never affected his loyalty to Col. Vaux and his battalion. It must be remembered that for the first six months of his service, the 7th was a front line fighting battalion. For example, the War Diary has the following entries:

> 21.5.15: In front line with 85th Brigade [28th Division]. 'A' and 'B' Companies attached to 3rd Battalion Royal Fusiliers between Bellevaarde and Ypres–Roulers Railway. Bn. HQ and 'C' and 'D' Companies attached to 3rd Battalion Middlesex Regiment between Ypres–Roulers Railway and Ypres–Verlorenhoek, relieving 20th

Hussars.

23.5.15: HQ, 'C' and 'D' Companies withdrawn to Brielen. 'A' and 'B' Companies remained with Royal Fusiliers.

24.5.15: 3 a.m. Gas clouds released by Germans, followed by bombardment and infantry attack. 3rd Royal Fusiliers and 'A' and 'B' Companies forced back to 2nd Line with heavy loss. Gas reached Bn HQ and 'C' and 'D' Companies. Respirators (cotton waste treated with Hypophosphate of soda) OK.

The 7th Battalion became the Divisional Pioneer Battalion on the 16th November 1915. The duties of a pioneer battalion were varied, and often onerous and dangerous, yet absolutely essential. It dug trenches and roadways, reinforced strong points and erected wire often in front of active enemy positions. The War Diary is evidence of the variety of work undertaken by the battalion:

1.1.16: Rivetting communication trenches and making special dugouts for machine guns.

17.1.16: Making special dugouts in the front line trenches.

21.1.16: Work on a new grenade school (Divisional) began in Dickesbusch Camp.

24.2.16: 2/Lt. Foster's party proceeded to Transport Farm to make the dummy assembly trenches. Brig. Shea showed them the place.

15–16.4.16: Repairing front line trench which was heavily bombarded each day.

Roland certainly did not waste his time in the 7th Battalion. In addition to his duties, he commenced 'spare time' activities that seemed to indicate that he was preparing himself for further promotion. He set out to improve his knowledge of the French language and started to learn Spanish. He trained his memory by reciting what he had read from a book, which he held behind his back. He practised his oral skills in the intimacy of his billet, standing in front of a mirror and speaking and moving his hands in appropriate gestures. There was a definite aim in these activities as later, when he commanded the 9th Battalion and 186 Brigade, he often spoke to his officers and men with stirring words which uplifted their spirits – pre dating Field Marshall Montgomery in the Second World War!

On the 26th September, the battalion moved to trenches northeast of Houplines for a period of patrolling and gathering intelligence about the enemy's defences. On the 13th November, it moved to billets near Bailleul and three days later became the Divisional Pioneer Battalion. Its movements, until Roland left it, included periods in Sanctuary Wood, The Bluff and Hill 60, areas that have become synonymous with some of the most intense battle of the First World War.

While George had a relatively quiet year at sea, his brothers had tested themselves against the enemy. For them, 1915 ended in routine if unpleasant trench duties, but 1916 would present new challenges for all the brothers.

Chapter 6

1916

A much more active year for most of the brothers, 1916 began with the second of the Bradfords' awards.

On the 14th January 1916, the *London Gazette* announced the award of the Distinguished Service Order to Capt. Thomas Andrews Bradford for service in the field. He had already been Mentioned In Despatches on two separate occasions.

During 1916, Thomas was promoted to Staff Captain and then Brigade Major. In addition to his award and promotion, another event had an impact on Thomas's life: while on leave in England, he married Honore Rebe Blackett, whom he would have known from the time when he served as a volunteer prior to the war. Both children of coalmine managers, Rebe and Thomas may have had much in common in terms of background and growing up. Certainly their ages were well matched: at the time of the wedding, she was 28 and Thomas 29.

Later in the year, Thomas took a regular commission with the York and Lancs Regiment and was sent to Ireland to join the 7th Young Officers Training Battalion as an instructor. This move may have been due to some wound that had rendered him unfit for front-line service, although there is no record of this. Whatever the reason, at Femoy in Ireland he was to spend some of the happiest years of his life. There was plenty of time to pursue some of his favourite pastimes: shooting, hunting and fishing. His wife Rebe was also with him, and he would not return from Ireland until the end of the war.

While Thomas was starting married life, his brother George was onboard the Orion and about to be tested in naval conflict. The Grand Fleet left its bases on the 30th May 1916 and sailed into what was to be known as the Battle of Jutland. HMS Orion and the Second Battle Squadron sailed from Cromarty in the Moray Firth and rendezvoused with the First Battle Squadron at a prearranged point in the North Sea. Intelligence had been received by the Admiralty that the German High Seas Fleet was at sea and the British Fleet concentrated to meet it. The British Cruiser Squadron (under Vice-Admiral Beatty) came upon the German Advanced Battle Cruiser Force (under Vice-Admiral Hipper) sometime after 3 p.m. on the 31st May. Neither of the combatants was aware that the respective Battle Fleets were approaching each other behind their cruiser screens. The British suffered the heavier losses in this initial encounter and Beatty broke off and drew the pursuing German forces after him and towards the approaching British Grand Fleet, commanded by Admiral Jellicoe.

HMS Orion, flying the flag of Rear Admiral Leveson, led the Second Division of the British Fleet. We can only imagine the excitement of the British

Captain Thomas Bradford, c. 1917.

crews at the prospect of at last meeting the enemy after so many frustrating months of inactivity. The Battle Fleets clashed just after 6 p.m.. In a classic manoeuvre executed by Jellicoe, the British battleships gained an initial advantage by crossing the 'T', meaning that they sailed across the enemy's path and were able to fire straight on the leading German vessels while not exposing themselves to dangerous broadside fire. HMS Orion was the fifth ship in line to come into action. She fired several salvoes at enemy ships of the German Third Battle Squadron and badly damaged the German Battle Cruiser Lutzow. The German Fleet turned away and managed to escape, due to a combination of delayed follow-up by the British and their lack of information as to the Germans' position and course. George Bradford had seen violent warfare at close hand for the first time. It was to remain his only experience until his selection for the Zeebrugge raid, which took place in April 1918.

The spring of 1916 was an eventful time for the other Bradfords who were in France. On the 11th March, the 18th Battalion Durham Light Infantry arrived in Marseilles from Egypt. At some point after its arrival in France, James joined the Battalion and was appointed Bombing Officer. The battalion moved up to the Somme front and went into the line on the 29th March, in the White City Sector, northwest of Beaumont Hamel. Here it alternated between the front line, at rest and the reserve positions in the area and adjusted to the appalling weather and trench conditions. On the 14th May, the battalion moved to the trenches in front of Serre and it remained in this area until the disastrous attack on the 1st July 1916.

On the 30th June 1916, 'D' Company of the 18th Battalion joined the 16th Battalion West Yorkshire Regiment in the front line. It was part of the first wave of the assault infantry that would go over the top on the following morning, 1st July, the opening day of the Battle of the Somme. The rest of 18th Battalion was in reserve. On reaching the reserve trenches at 4.50 a.m. on the 1st July, special bombing parties under the command of Second Lieutenant James Bradford moved up to the assault trenches to assist the 15th Battalion, West Yorkshire Regiment. At 7.30 a.m. that morning, the British infantry came out of the front line trenches and were met by a storm of German shell and machine gun fire. Most of the attacking battalions in front of Serre were killed or wounded within the first few yards. The survivors of 'D' Company disappeared into Pendant Copse, never to be seen again. What happened to James Bradford and his bombing parties or what part they played on the day is not known. Unlike the very great majority of his comrades, he had seen bitter fighting in the Ypres Salient and, no doubt, he called upon that experience to meet the demands of the day. James's experience would have been of great value in leading his men, most of whom had not yet fired a shot in anger. Casualties in the bombing parties are not known, but on that day the British suffered 60,000 casualties, 19,000 of which were killed outright. James survived the ordeal.

James at Milbanke House, 1916. A nurse was on hand through his convalescent leave.

A period of rest followed. New drafts were received and training began. On the 27th July, the battalion went into the line in the Neuve Chappelle Sector, an area already well known to James. On the first day in the trenches, they were subjected to fierce enemy artillery fire, which was followed by infantry attacks. The fighting continued until the Germans were finally driven off, but not before James was wounded. On the 1st August, James received gunshot wounds to arm and right ankle. He was sent back to England and spent several weeks at the family home in Darlington on convalescent leave.

While at home recovering, James married Annie Wall of Darlington in the late summer. When and how he met Nancy – the name by which she was always known – and how their courtship developed is not known. She had attended his sister Amy's private boarding school at Wycombe Abbey, though senior to his sister. A local girl, James may have known her through mutual connections in Darlington. In the few letters in which she is mentioned, Nancy appears to have been accepted by the family as a valued member. James rejoined his battalion on the Somme front in mid-October 1916.

The spring and summer of 1916 also saw changes for Roland. While in the Kemmel area on the 8th May, Roland was promoted to Temporary Major and transferred as Second in Command to the 9th Battalion The Durham Light

Infantry. He was just 24. In a note upon his leaving, Lt. Co. Vaux wrote to Roland:

> Our year together has been, in my opinion, a very wonderful one. Never since you joined me have you and I had a single wrong word, and honestly I feel deeply all the things you have done for me.

Roland's new battalion, the 9th Durham Light Infantry, was commanded by Lt. Col. W.B. Moir. When he joined the battalion it was in rest billets near Westroutre, in the southern sector of the Ypres Salient. Roland wrote to his brother Thomas with typical humour:

> We are resting now, near the place where you were in hospital just before you left...I am a Temporary Major – so mind you click your heels smartly when you next see me!

The 9th Battalion was part of 151 Brigade of the 50th Northumbrian Infantry Division. It, too, had its baptism of fire within a few short days of arriving in France and Belgium. By April 1916, one year after arriving in France, the battalion had lost a total of 50 officers and 1,264 NCOs and men, the equivalent of an entire battalion. The 151 Brigade was commanded by Brig. Gen. J.S.M. Shea and was affectionately known as 'Jimmy Shea's Tigers'. Brig. Gen. Shea left the brigade in May to take command of the 30th Division, just as Roland was arriving. Brig. Gen. P.F. Westmoreland succeeded as Shea's replacement.

The 9th Battalion remained at rest near Westroutre from the 8th to the 26th May. It was in training during this period, and may have noticed a few changes due to the new Second in Command. Training was central to Roland's military philosophy, and he and his officers laid down a schedule that was hard and demanding, with an emphasis on physical fitness. Anything expected of the troops, however, was also expected of the officers, and Roland led the way to prove that they would be at least as fit as his men.

On the 27th May, the 9th Battalion relieved the 7th Battalion Shropshire Light Infantry in the Vieerstraat sector. For the next seven days in the front line, the battalion patrolled no man's land, and much damage was done to the opposing trenches by heavy shelling and mortaring. Casualties remained light. The battalion was relieved by the 6th Battalion Durham Light Infantry on the 2nd June, and it proceeded to rest billets and into divisional reserve. It returned to the line on the 8th of the month for a further seven-day stretch. On the 15th the *London Gazette* announced that Maj. R.B. Bradford had been Mentioned In Despatches for the second time.

Through his achievements, Roland was beginning to build a name for himself. Col. W.D.B. Thompson DSO, MC, was one of Roland's officers. In his unpublished manuscript, *The Boy General – A Life of Brigadier General Roland Boys Bradford*, Col. Thompson records an anecdote of Roland's no-nonsense reputation:

> It so happened that a 2nd Lieut. posted from the 3/9th Bn. D.L.I. at Rothbury,

Northumberland, arrived in France at the beginning of June 1916 and joined the Bn., where he was sent to 'B' Coy...On the following night, when 'B' Coy. had taken over the front line trenches (M & N) the subaltern was ordered to take out a patrol (of 3 men) into No Man's Land when darkness fell and see what, if anything, was going on and report back. Setting out into the unknown for the first time, the patrol eventually made their way back to our trenches. There, waiting on the parapet, was R.B. Bradford, who quietly told the subaltern, he had not been out long enough to report fully on this situation in No Man's Land. The subaltern, a bit set back by this, his first experience of night patrolling and trench warfare, said he would go out again. However, this time he provided himself with a pair of wire cutters. Now, the pattern of the German and British 'barbs' was entirely different and so, when the subaltern got back nearly as dawn was breaking, he was again met by R.B. Bradford, to whom he produced the sample of the enemy barbed wire.

A smiling Roland in France, c. 1916

For the following month, Roland and his battalion alternated in and out of the front line trenches. In the line, they were shelled and mortared almost daily. Out of it, they formed working parties and spent most nights in the usual manner of working parties – repairing roads, fortifying trenches, transporting materials, fixing wiring and the like. On the 19th July they moved into the Kemmel sector. On the 8th August, the whole division was withdrawn from the front line and prepared to move down to the Somme. Just days before, on the 4th August, Roland had been given command of the 9th Battalion. Roland wrote to his mother on the 17th:

I hope you are quite well. I have just heard from Tommy and he tells me that George is coming home on leave. I wish I was. But 'roll on' as the Tommies say.

I am now commanding my battalion and I hope to be made a Lieutenant Colonel soon. I will not have much opportunity for writing for a few days so don't expect a letter. We are in a very pleasant part of France and the weather is delightful.

In August 1916 Roland was promoted to Acting Lieutenant Colonel. His substantive rank was still that of Lieutenant. More than his letter home indicates, it was this promotion that was the making of Roland Boys Bradford, and of the 9th Battalion.

Under Roland, the 9th became one of the finest battalions in the British army. Known for its 'esprit de corps', much of the battalion's efficiency and camaraderie can be traced to Roland's leadership and the keen interest he took in the well being of his men. Capt. M. Jolley MC, served with Roland as a platoon commander and later a company commander, and he had the following to say about his commanding officer:

> He was a great personality, so very efficient in every way, and always able to deal with any emergency which happened to arise. We never went into action without knowing exactly what our objective was, and the Operation Orders were always issued to the Coy. Commanders in good time so every Officer and Other Ranks were fully informed before the day of attack. Colonel Bradford was a very clever tactician, and above all a very brave soldier, which made him a great leader in the eyes of all who served under him....I think one outstanding point in his character, was his unfailing endeavours to see his troops had always, as far as possible, food, clothing comforts in the Line, and decent billets when we were out in Rest. Well do I remember how he used to come round and personally inspect every billet of the whole Battalion before he went to his own.

Maj. E.H. Veitch MC (serving with the 8th Battalion DLI) also knew Roland and wrote:

> He had an extraordinary charming personality. His smile and greeting on meeting you actually made you feel that there was nothing he liked better than to see you. His first thought for everyone, officers and men, was their comfort. His attention for detail was extraordinary. He saw to everything himself, even to supervising a working party.

William Herdman, who served in the battalion office, was witness to how far Roland would go to ensure his men's needs were met when he wrote:

> He [Bradford] wrote to Headquarters stating, 'My men must have their fair share of jam in order to fight'. Next day, 'My men must have cheese', then 'bread', and finished the series, 'My men have to rely on daily news reports while newspapers are circulating daily in all rear areas', and he requested immediate attention and some real responsive action.

> The Divisional General duly appeared and Col. Bradford met him at the entrance to our Orderly Room, a cleaned two-stall stable. After salutations the General told the C.O. to relax, but he stood like a ram-rod. The General said he had ready the 'silly' letters (whoops!). The C.O. said the contents were a fact and true...We got more cheese, jam and also newspapers.

Roland's letters were well noted for his frankness. A fellow officer observed:

> He appeared rather tactless in his official letters, but his nature was well understood at Brigade and Divisional headquarters. It was always realised that he was so much wrapped up in the subject of his letters that he never considered what they would appear like to others. And even if remonstrated he always had the courage to stick to his opinions.

Roland's confrontation regarding rations was just one of the times he took on higher authority for the welfare of his men. It was well known that if Roland thought he was right, nothing would shake him. The family book tells of conversation with the General:

> [Roland] was always thinking about leave for his men, and urging that more of them should be sent on leave. Things approached something in the nature of a crisis when a General paid a visit to the 9th. Without hesitation, Roland tackled him on the subject of leave, and during the course of the conversation frankly stated that the leave which ought to go to the fighting troops was taken by the staff behind the lines. This remark not unnaturally caused the subsequent conversation to be more than a little animated. For a long time, we are told, the General eyed Bradford up and down as though he would place him under arrest, and then told him that, 'Leave for the men was his first consideration and leave was properly allotted'.

> Roland, however, refused to be convinced, and it was perhaps fortunate that the man with whom he was dealing had a considerable knowledge of human nature and some sense of humour. For this incident ended in the General patting Roland on the back and remarking that he was damned glad someone was as interested in the men's leave as he himself was.

We are not told the identity of the General, but Rodney Gee (who was to be Roland's Battalion Adjutant) remembered him as the Corps Commander.

Borne out of his concern for the well being of his men, Roland strove to make the 9th one of the best-prepared fighting battalions in the British Army. One of the ways he saw to achieve this was to exercise strict discipline in every way. Roland was especially particular about appearance – of his men and their environment. The men had to shave each day, whether in or out of the line. Hair had to be cut short. Roland showed the way with a short-cropped haircut, and he was always clean-shaven and immaculately presented. Trenches, too, had to be spotless. Cigarette ends, paper, tins, jars and so on were cleared up immediately after use. Toilet paper was issued to replace the use of addressed envelopes and scraps of paper, which, if blown in the wind towards the enemy lines, may have revealed that the Durhams were now in the opposite trenches. The trenches became a hive of activity if it was known that Roland was on his way. There was a purpose in all this: in the damp, cramped conditions of the trenches, disease was never far away. Every effort to improve health and hygiene was taken seriously. Men wore sandbags on their legs in the trenches instead of their puttees. When these got dirty, they could be changed and dug into the wall of the trench. With regard to his own appearance, Roland showed a good example by being immaculately presented. He was also easily recognisable in transit or parade, seated on an identifiable grey charger.

The limited edition family book relates one of his orders with regard to health:

> Watching closely over the health of the men, he [Roland] had been impressed by the amount of skin disease that existed among them. So he consulted the Regimental Medical Officer and, having been assured that Sun Bathing would be beneficial for the

disease, he issued an order that the men, whether in the line or resting, should sit naked in the sun for an hour each day. At first the modesty of the men prevented them of approving of his command,   but Roland never expected any man to do a thing that he was not prepared to do himself and, after he had given them a lead, the difficulty very soon was not to get them to take off their clothes but to see that they put them on again at the end of the hour.

This order may seem unusual, but the health of men coming into the army had been an eye-opener for the authorities. Many were unfit, undernourished and showed a range of diseases directly linked to poverty – skin disease being one of them. Living in the trenches, men were unable to change clothing, and their dirty uniforms attracted lice and exacerbated skin conditions. Given Roland's long held views on good health, he would undoubtedly have wanted to address this problem, and if sunbathing was the advice of the medical officer, he would have been sure to act upon it. There is some controversy about the extent of the nudity stipulated; Second Lieutenant Gee, who became Roland's Adjutant in 1917, claimed in a later interview that the men were not ordered to strip naked but merely to remove their shirts and vests. Whatever the extent, the order has incited speculation about Roland's sexuality, though there is no evidence to support any claim. In Roland's own day, there was certainly no discussion of sexual orientation; while the modern military may have a more liberal attitude to homosexuality, even a rumour in early years of the last century could have destroyed the career of a young officer like Roland.

Roland's concern for his troops meant that when he was in the trenches, he spent a few hours of every day talking to the men. It was sometimes felt that some regular soldiers of the battalion knew the Commander's mind better than his officers. Capt. H.C.B. Plummer MC, the Battalion Intelligence Officer wrote:

> He often spoke to his battalion before or after an engagement and, on one occasion, I remember him telling them not to be ashamed to pray.

Col. Thompson observed Roland's reticence with officers:

> To company officers, he was not very communicative on matters other than the opera-
> tions in hand. He was always 'up with the company'; either in reserve areas, trenches,
> and especially in attack. In discussing operations he was concise and lucidly explained
> any situation. As company officers came to meet him, he could be described as austere
> but moodiness was never part of his nature….He was known to make his devotions in
> his tent when the battalion was out of the trenches…fear was never in his nature.

Capt. M. Jolley recalled Roland's familiarity with his men:

> He also had a marvellous memory, being able to name anyone in the whole unit upon
> his approach whether a Private or NCO, when inspecting the various companies out at
> Rest. I do not think he ever showed a great sense of humour, his aim in life was to be a
> real soldier and leader of men. This he certainly did accomplish and the whole
> Battalion was behind him in all he did…
>
> As far as I remember, Colonel Bradford was not a great socialite, he spent a good deal

of time in his own company when possible, perhaps he preferred it that way.

The men who served under Roland appreciated his interest, and went to great lengths to show their respect. Col. Thompson recorded a time, probably during the coming winter, when Roland's men perhaps went a bit too far to show their appreciation:

> We have noted that R.B. Bradford had a very good looking grey gelding. Well he also found himself a second charger....
>
> It was a cold winter's day and alongside the 9th DLI horse lines were the lines of an Australian Battalion. Taken out into the freezing atmosphere from the warmth of a bell tent, the Transport Officer pointed out that a few transport lads of the 9th Battalion were having a hell of an argument near the Australian horse lines. Of course a fight broke out in which the Australian transport chaps gathered round and cheered on the combatants. Then from shall we say the shadows two quiet lads of 9 DLI transport worked quietly through the Australian horse lines and gently led away a beautiful light chestnut...I do not think for a moment that R.B.B. ever did know why his second charger was called "Anzac".

For Roland, his men came first and woe betide any officer in the battalion who placed his own needs before those of the men. His excellent company of officers was a testament to his high expectations, and he was quick to dismiss those who did not make the grade. Second Lieutenant Gee recalled the first time he heard of Roland, from a few officers who had been dismissed:

> When I was going on leave, I shared a carriage with two officers who had been dismissed by Bradford after a few days, being incompetent or unfit to be officers. They told me a bit about him. Very fiercesome... I'd never heard of him before.

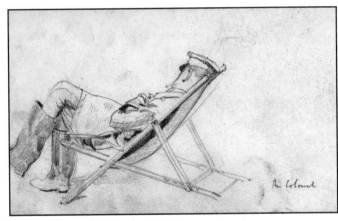

Roland Bradford catching some sleep; sketched from life by Capt. R. Mauchlen MC, 1916.

They also advised Lt. Gee to have his long hair cut before he reported to Bradford. On route to joining the battalion, the young Second Lieutenant received a further warning from some others who had experience of Roland's 9th:

> On the way up on the train, some officers returning from leave said, 'Where are you going?' I said, '9 D.L.I.' 'Whew! Well you've got hell in front of you!'...I had been told if he punished anybody, he always gave them the maximum punishment, 28 days. He knew all by name and spent a lot of time talking to them. Certainly, when in the trenches, he spent all day with them. I hardly saw him...He could tick people off.

Swearing? No. Only 'bloody', never seriously…He was difficult and the betting was that I would not last a month.

As it happened the young officer hit it off with Roland from the very beginning and he served as his Adjutant for most of the time that Roland was with the battalion. Second Lieutenant Gee, like all the officers who stayed with the battalion, had to meet exacting standards, even in relatively small matters. On taking over as Adjutant in 1917, Gee stated:

Bradford made me change my handwriting…he said, 'Your writing may be very beautiful but you must be like Corporal So-and-So'. Eventually after a month or so he said, 'Did you or Corporal So-and-So write this?' I said, 'I wrote it'…But I spent hours of the days standing to attention, watching him dealing with this, that or the other. Very often he would say, 'There's an order, lose it!' I would look at it and lose it….Anything futile he just ignored….He was strong enough with his VC and MC to get away with a lot.

Roland's officers tended to be young like himself. Second Lieutenant Gee recalled:

He wanted young people and would work them, if they were suitable, work them almost to death. If they were` good they would get a company…If they seemed tired, he would get them a soft job, or send them on a course to Boulogne or somewhere. It was like a fortnight's holiday.

Capt. H.C.B. Plummer MC, Roland's Intelligence Officer, observed:

While realising the privileges due to officers, he believed that they ought to share certain discomforts with the men, notably the carrying of a pack on the march. If the men were wearing steel helmets he invariably wore his and once when he was returning to the battalion, he borrowed a runners steel helmet, so that he might take the salute, 'properly dressed', as he called it. To junior officers particularly he was always willing to give advice and help and many, like myself, have every reason to be grateful to him.

Roland relied heavily on his good officers and his sergeants, particularly the latter. The sergeants formed the backbone of the battalion and, almost without exception, were first class. They were carefully selected. Some were quite young and all had immense pride in the battalion and a great trust in their young leader. Second Lieutenant Gee remembered:

His attitude was that the men were more important – their morale, their skill, their spirit could make up for poor officers.

Principal among Roland's officers was his Second in Command, Maj. Crouch DCM. Maj. Crouch was from London and had enlisted in the 1st Battalion Durham Light Infantry in 1891. Col. W.D.B. Thompson later wrote of him:

He served with the Mounted Infantry Company of the 2nd Battalion in the South African War, being severely wounded, and by the outbreak of the Great War was attached to the 9th Battalion as Regimental Sergeant Major, and went to France with them in that capacity. His service in that war is a saga in itself; commissioned in the Field in 1915; Distinguished Conduct Medal gazetted in 1916; Distinguished Service Order 1917; five times mentioned in despatches, and awarded the French Legion of Honour.

Maj. Crouch was an archetypical old soldier: dour, solid and reliable, with considerable experience. A perfect foil for his young commander, he and Roland soon developed a relationship based on mutual respect, and Roland owed much to the support and wise counsel of the experienced Crouch. Col. Thompson wrote:

And so in the bloody days of 1916–17, the 9th Battalion had at its head two regular soldiers. From this amalgamation of a young regular subaltern and a warrant officer of South African War experience, they together with their regimental training and background, developed a battalion trained to the highest standards with a fighting tenacity, loyalty, moral honesty, all of which was freely and proudly given by the lads from Gateshead-on-Tyne and nearby townships and villages in the Battalion recruiting area.

Another outstanding officer at battalion headquarters when Roland took command was the Adjutant, Capt. R. Boys Stones. He was awarded the Military Cross in 1916 and a Bar in 1918. He was twice Mentioned In Despatches and twice wounded. The Battalion Medical Officer was Maj. J.A.C. Scott. Col. Thompson wrote of him:

Completing Bradford's H.Q. Staff was the Medical Officer, Major J.A.C. Scott, known inevitably as 'Doc'. Like his 'patients' in the 9th, Dr. Scott came from Gateshead, where his father had been Master at the Workhouse. He left his practice in the town to accompany the battalion to France, where his quiet manner and Geordie voice dispelled many fears amongst the wounded and dying. He too was much decorated, being awarded the Military Cross with two Bars and the French Croix de Guerre avec Palme.

The skilled officers, discipline, morale and training that Roland brought to the 9th would shortly be tested in battle. On the 8th August 1916, Roland's battalion and the 50th Division came out of the line, and prepared to move south to take part in the Battle of the Somme, which had been raging since the 1st July 1916.

Chapter 7

Roland and The Somme

James had experienced the horrific opening day of the Battle of the Somme. By the time Roland got there, the Somme was well established as a killing ground that had decimated an entire generation of young volunteers.

On the 11th August, the 9th Battalion entrained at Godewaersvelde and detrained at Candas, about 20 miles north of Albert. From here they marched seven miles to Prouville, arriving at 2 a.m. on the following morning. Between the 15th and the 17th, the battalion marched via Vignacourt and Rainville to Baisieux, a distance of some 28 miles. For this trek, it was congratulated by the Brigade Commander on being the best marching battalion in the brigade. The battalion billeted in Baisieux Wood; officers in a few tents and the men in bivouacs made of waterproof sheets, branches and brushwood. The entire 50th Division was in the surrounding villages. Training commenced immediately, though much was frustrated by the heavy rains that set in. After 16 months in trenches, Roland's men were not as fit as required. Soft feet had to be remedied; marching and toughening-up exercises quickly brought about the desired change. Roland read the army reports and almost certainly talked to fellow officers from other battalions who had come out of the front line, and he would have considered their advice and experiences in his training activities. Training included attacking replica trenches and holding them against the inevitable German counter-attack.

On the 10th September, the battalion moved to Becourt Wood and on the 14th, it marched to Mametz Wood where it bivouacked in the southwest corner. The brigade was now in divisional reserve and was expected to attack on the following day. The men were in high spirits and anxious to meet the enemy, though the devastation of the battlefield in general and Mametz Wood in particular must have been somewhat sobering. The wood had been bitterly fought over, and the few trees that remained standing were splintered stumps. Trenches criss-crossed the wood and many of the dead remained unburied in the undergrowth. Men sheltered in the small hollows they found or could dig as enemy shells continued to fall around them. No fires could be lit nor lights shown.

On the 15th September, with tanks used for the first time in military history though none on the front of 151 Brigade, a series of attacks were launched to drive the Germans from the ridge. On the right, the 47th Division was now in possession of one half of High Wood. On the left, the 15th Scottish Division held the line southwest of Martinpuich. Both of these divisions were in positions sited some 300 yards to the rear of those held by the 50th Division. In fact, the 50th occupied a salient between the two and could be subjected to enemy enfilade fire from both flanks. The line the 50th held rested on Sutherland Trench, a communication trench running north-south that joined Clark's Trench where it met the Bazentin-le-Petit–High Wood road. The line then ran to the west along Clark's Trench and Swansea Trench to join up with the right flank of the 15th Scottish Division. Throughout the 50th's territory, the ground held was in an appalling state, little more than a tangle of trenches, roads and tracks, rutted with innumerable shell holes and craters.

In front of the 50th Division, there were three lines of trenches. The first objective was Hook Trench. The second objective comprised Martin Trench, The Bow and The Starfish Line. The latter continued to form the third objective with Pru Trench, which ran east and southeast from Martinpuich.

Rather than wait until the two flanking divisions came up level with his brigades, Maj. Gen. Wilkinson GOC 50th Division decided to attack immediately when the general assault began. His attacking brigades were 149 on the right and 150 on the left, with 151 Brigade in reserve. The General reasoned that by advancing he could threaten the rear of the German positions, thus assisting the two other attacking British divisions. In fact, the battle played out much differently – and worse – than the General planned. Once out in the open, both brigades were subjected to heavy enemy flanking fire and experienced extreme losses for little gain.

At 6.30 a.m., the attacking brigades climbed out of their trenches toward the enemy positions. The objective of 149 Brigade was Hook Trench, and it attacked with the 4th Bn. Northumberland Fusiliers on the right and its sister battalion the 7th on the left. Hook Trench was captured at about 7 a.m. The Northumberland Fusiliers moved on to their next objective, which was part of the Starfish Line. The attack was timed for 7.20 a.m. but it started late. Intense enemy flanking fire had already cost many lives. The 47th Division was still in High Wood and unable to move in support. The sunken road south of The Bow was reached but by now few men remained on their feet and they were exhausted. It was at this point in the battle that the 9th Battalion was called forward to continue the advance. It was its first major attack under the command of Roland Bradford.

At 6.20 a.m., Roland led the battalion from the southwest corner of High Wood to the northwest corner. At noon, it was attached to 149 Brigade. He moved two of his companies to Mill Street and two to Chalk Road, with battalion headquarters in the quarry [map reference S8d 9.9]. At 3 p.m., the battalion was called forward to Hook Trench, with battalion headquarters in Clark's Trench, and orders to attack at 6 p.m. 'B' Company of the Divisional Pioneers, the 7th Battalion DLI, was attached to make communication trenches between successive lines. This attack was cancelled, much to the frustration of the battalion and Roland. The attack was rescheduled for 9.00 p.m. The battalion War Diary recorded:

At 9.00 p.m. the Battalion in conjunction with the 5th Border Regiment and 6 DLI was to attack the German Starfish and Pru Lines. The 5th Borders and 6 DLI were late in starting [held up by the appalling state of the ground they had to cross]. Our Battalion was met with heavy machine gun fire and rifle fire from both flanks. Part of the first two waves crossed the Starfish Line and pushed on to about 30 yards from Pru Trench and dug in there, these small parties were all killed with exception of four wounded men who crawled back. Those who had entered the Starfish Line were ejected and our front line dug itself in on a line M34c 2.6 to M34c 5.4 [map reference] and consolidated a line there.

While up with the attacking companies, Roland was hit by a piece of shrapnel and received a nasty wound. Second in Command Maj. Crouch wrote:

…the tenacious spirit of the C.O., which would not be denied the honour of leading his battalion into action, kept him on duty. What he suffered physically by this noble act he alone knew, but I do know that two months later it was still necessary for the M.O. to dress his wounds.

A further attack was planned for the following day and the battalion commanders of 151 Brigade met the Brigadier that evening. An unnamed officer of another battalion who was present wrote:

At a meeting of the COs at 8.30 p.m. on that day [15th September], Bradford was present and said little. A plan of attack was being drawn up by the Brigadier and the hour he had first fixed was, I think, 10 [a.m.]. At this point Bradford spoke and said he thought it was too early. It was put off until, I think, 10.30… Bradford during the attack was up in the front line of his battalion and back in Clark's Trench and continually moving about with the most surprising vigour. He went forward with one attack and carried a wounded man back under heavy fire to the assembly trench.

This officer's memory of the timing of the attack was faulty, for it began on the following morning at 9.30 a.m.

The 9th's assault on the Starfish Line, accompanied by the 5th Border Regiment, failed again due to the intensity of the enemy machine gun and rifle fire from both the front and the flanks. On the 17th, Roland ordered Second Lieutenants Bowdery and Thompson to take 50 men and attack once again. The attack commenced at 10.30 p.m. but was again held up be heavy enemy machine gun and rifle fire. The survivors established a number of posts in shell holes about 100 yards in front of the battalion's position. A further attack was made on the following day, supported by Capt. Oswald's company of the 8th Battalion. This, too, was unsuccessful. At 8 p.m., the 9th Battalion was relieved and withdrew to Clark's Trench and into reserve. It had suffered grievous casualties over the last three days: 4 officers were killed or died of wounds, 9 were wounded; 44 other ranks were killed, 27 were missing and 219 were wounded. This was 44% of the battalion's strength that had gone into action.

On the 20th September, the battalion moved to Mametz Wood where it furnished working parties and received a draft of 23 reinforcements. Work continued until the 28th when it moved back into the line and, during the night, dug a fire trench and a communication trench. As a testament to the origins of the battalion, the fire trench was christened Blaydon Trench and the communication trench Chopwell Avenue. It was relieved on the 29th by the 6th DLI and moved back into Pru Trench and the Starfish Line, which had eventually fallen to successive British attacks during the preceding days.

The 6th Battalion was holding the line in the Eaucourt L'Abbay sector, with the 47th Division on its right, and a composite battalion of the 8th DLI and the 5th Borders on its left. The 9th DLI was in close support of the 6th Battalion. The 47th Division had again failed to come up on the right and there was an open flank in this position. A heavy British bombardment of the enemy lines commenced on the 30th September and continued through to the next day. Also on the 30th, the battalion received a telegram from the Divisional Commander, Maj. Gen. Wilkinson (which had been endorsed by the Brigade Commander), congratulating the battalion 'for their gallant work during the last 48 hours'.

An attack was planned for 3.15 p.m. on the afternoon of the 1st October. The attacking 6th Battalion experienced a major setback at 1.30 p.m., when its commanding officer Maj. Wilkinson was wounded by enemy shellfire. It went into action without him, led by junior officers. Maj. Wilkinson had made his way back to the casualty clearing station to have his wounds treated. He wrote:

> On my way back I went in and saw Colonel Bradford and his Adjutant at his headquarters at Seven Elms and told him of the situation and I suggested to him that he should go up and take command of the 6th DLI in addition to the 9th. I told him that it was imperative to have a senior officer up to control matters, as I had no one in my battalion except Lieutenants and 2nd Lieutenants.
>
> I, then, proceeded on my way back and met the Brigadier and Brigade Major two miles behind, coming up to their Battle Headquarters and I told him what I had arranged with Colonel Bradford and he immediately approved my action.

The 6th Battalion advanced under enemy shellfire and entered the first German line of trenches. Roland, having been given permission by the Brigadier to take command of the 6th Battalion, crossed the open ground, which was under heavy enemy shellfire and joined the attacking battalion. The 6th had suffered heavy losses and he quickly ordered forward two of the 9th Battalion's companies to reinforce it. With the added strength, the 6th advanced, taking the German second line by 1 a.m. on the 2nd October. With the right flank still open, blocks were established in both lines and fierce fighting took place at these vulnerable points. The enemy were unable to break in at either of the blocks. If they had been successful, then the whole British line would have come under concentrated enfilade fire and attack. The possibility of the enemy rolling up the British front was clear. The battalion War Diary entry reads:

> Bomb fighting of a severe nature raged round our blocks on our right flank for 24 hrs., but all attempts to eject us were repulsed. On our gaining both our first and second objectives, touch was immediately established with the 5th Borders and 8 DLI on our left.

Roland was at the forefront of the action at the trench blocks. His towering presence, personal courage, tactics, leadership and his ability to encourage his troops to great effort did so much to win the day and the enemy failed to make an entry. An enemy counter-attack was beaten off. Patrols were sent forward and found strongly held enemy positions ahead, particularly in the maze of trenches known as 'The Tangle'. As the 47th Division had failed to appear on the right, it was obvious no further advance could be made. The position was consolidated in spite of heavy enemy attacks and shelling during the 2nd October.

Roland was awarded the Victoria Cross for his leadership in this action. His citation read:

> Lieut. (temporary Lieut-Col.) Roland Boys Bradford, MC, Durham Light Infantry, for most conspicuous bravery and good leadership in attack, whereby he saved the situation on the right flank of his brigade and of the division. Lt. Col. Bradford's battalion was in support. A leading battalion having suffered very severe casualties and the commander being wounded, its flank became dangerously exposed at close quarters to the enemy. Raked by machine gun fire, the situation of the battalion became critical. At the request of the wounded commander, Lt. Col. Bradford asked permission to command the exposed battalion in addition to his own. Permission granted, he at once proceeded to the foremost lines. By his fearless conduct under fire of all description and his skilful leadership of the two battalions, regardless of all danger, he succeeded in rallying the attack, captured and defended the objective and so secured the flank.

The report of Maj. Wilkinson and Roland's citation differ slightly: Maj. Wilkinson says he suggested Roland should take command of the 6th; the citation states that Roland volunteered for this responsibility. Whatever the truth, the actions are accurate. Maj. Veitch, of the 8th DLI, wrote:

> Lt. Col. Bradford was first recommended for the DSO by Brig. Gen. Cameron (151 Bde.) but as full details of his action became known this recommendation was withdrawn and he was recommended for the VC instead. On the 1st October, immediately after the successful attack I went to his Headquarters at 'Seven Elms' about half a mile in front of High Wood. Col. Bradford had only a very short time before returned from leading the attack, and I was astonished to find him looking as though he had 'just stepped out of his tailors'. Looking at him it was difficult to realise that less than an hour before he had been in the thick of the fighting. It was all in keeping with his strong belief in the morale effect of his presence and appearance on those who he came into contact with. He certainly inspired confidence in everyone who saw him at that time when things were decidedly uncomfortable, and very uncertain. It was a little thing, but I came away feeling that everything was alright. In other words, 'It did all of us good to see him.'

Maj. Veitch is wrong about the date of his visit to the 9th Battalion's headquarters at 'Seven Elms'. It must have been the 2nd October, as Roland was fighting with his men throughout the night of the 1st October and into the following day.

Roland gave his own account of the battle in late autumn, when he wrote to Lord Northbourne, Honorary Colonel of the 9th Battalion:

I write to let you know the doings of the Battalion during the Somme offensive.

We went into the battle first on the 15th September, when we assisted in taking the enemy trenches between High Wood and Martinpuich. After a fortnight's hard fighting our Division captured the Flers front and support lines.

The men of this Battalion fought conspicuously well and with great gallantry. In all we had 70 officers and men killed and 400 wounded…The men are all happy and fit and eager to meet the accursed Germans.

Even though Roland would be awarded a VC for his bravery in this action, he modestly makes no mention of himself. Of course, he would not have known about the VC himself until it was announced on 25th November, but even if he did, we may suspect his usual modesty would have prevented him from mentioning it. Instead, Roland uses the opportunity of a letter to the Honorary Colonel to improve day-to-day life for his men. The letter continues:

I sent you a reproduction of a drawing of the Cross I had erected N.W. of High Wood in memory of the officers and men of the 9th DLI who fell in the Somme offensive. I have organised a Band, which is a great boon to all ranks. I know you will have a great many claims on you just now, but I venture to ask for one or two things. First of all I enclose a list of music which perhaps you could see your way to obtaining and sending to us. Do you think that during the winter you could send out a weekly parcel for the men of say, polonies, cakes, kippers, condensed milk and a few socks?

In the cold weather the great thing is to be able to feed the inner man.

Candles, too are very acceptable…

The band mentioned was the battalion band, which Roland had formed in mid-October – not without opposition from higher authority who decreed that musical instruments were well down the order of necessary supplies to be sent out from England. Aware that a number of men in the battalion could play musical instruments, and some had played in their local Salvation Army bands, Roland badgered his seniors until he succeeded in getting musical instruments as gifts from County Durham. An anonymous witness wrote:

Roland had a cross erected in High Wood to commemorate the dead, and later had these cards printed and distributed to the men of the 9th DLI. The signature is Roland's own.

The band played a great part in the training and morale structure of the Battalion.

On one occasion when the Battalion was somewhere near the town of Cassel, head-quarters of Gen. Plumer who commanded the Second Army, the Battalion marched through the streets of this small hillside town. With the Band and Drums playing the Companies marched to attention at the trail. It must have done the Second Army Headquarters good to behold such a well-trained Battalion with Roland Boys Bradford at its head on his famous grey charger.

Roland was extremely keen on anything that would cheer his men and keep their spirits up. To this effect, he also formed a theatrical group he named the 'Green Diamonds', who would perform skits, comedy and short plays. A new private starting with Roland's battalion observed:

I was in close touch with him [Roland] from December 1916 to April 1917, he being then C.O. of the 9th Battalion of the Durham Light Infantry. For although I was only a private, I saw a lot of him in connection with the formation of a 'Battalion Concert Party', which he proudly labelled 'The Green Diamonds'.

In his untiring efforts to bring some sunshine into the precarious lives of the men under his charge, he quickly discovered, on my joining his battalion, that my civilian occupation was that of an actor and he promptly sent for me. And he did not rest until the first performance of the Green Diamonds at Marycourt was a fait accompli.

On the 3rd October, the battalion was relieved by the 7th Bn. Northumberland Fusiliers. The relief took eight hours to come from Pru Trench, due to the appalling weather. The battalion returned to Bécourt Wood as part of the relief of the 50th Division by the 23rd Division. On the following day, it moved to Hénincourt Wood and into an excellent camp to spend its time refitting, receiving new drafts and training. On the 23rd of the month, it moved back to Bécourt Wood and into tents. It rained heavily for two days. On the 25th, the 50th Division relieved the 9th Scottish Division in the front line with 150 and 149 Brigades in the line and 151 Brigade in reserve in Mametz Wood. On the follow-ing day, Roland and his company commanders carried out a reconnaissance of the front line held by the battalion. The left divisional boundary was on the Martinpuich–Warlencourt road, the right boundary north of Eaucourt L'Abbaye. There was an attack planned for the 28th, but it was postponed due to bad weath-er. Persistent rain had turned no man's land into a quagmire of deep, clinging mud, and the many shell holes had filled with water. On the 3rd November, it moved into the line and into Maxwell Trench, Tail Trench and Snag Trench. Immediately in front lay the Butte de Warlencourt.

Maj. E.H. Veitch MC of the 8th Battalion DLI described the Butte:

The Gird Trench ran east and west from the Albert–Bapaume road towards Gueudecourt. On the left lay the Butte de Warlencourt, a mound or tumulus some forty feet high, reported to be an ancient burial-place similar to those found on Salisbury Plain. This, in September, when the Battalion first entered the Somme fighting, stood out from the surrounding country a green, conical-shaped hill. Of little or no strategic importance, except that it provided observation of all ground towards High Wood,

Martinpuich and east of that village, it had been so battered by the daily shelling that all signs of vegetation had now disappeared and it stood a shapeless, pockmarked mass of chalk. Beyond the Gird lay a stretch of undulating country with Bapaume clearly visible in the distance, and midway, almost hidden in a small valley, Le Barque. The remainder of the attack frontage held no special feature except a considerable amount of dead ground to the rear of the objective.

The Butte lay, however, in the path of the British advance towards Bapaume. The possibility of going round the Butte and isolating it to be mopped up later does not seemed to have occurred to the planners of this attack. Rather, it was planned to take the Butte by frontal assault in the most appalling conditions that any infantry could have been asked to attack in. The muddy ground, torn by shellfire and churned into a deep porridge by heavy rain, was from knee to thigh deep. This was to be crossed by infantry carrying heavy loads. The attack by 151 Brigade was planned for 9.10 a.m. on the 5th November, with 8th Battalion on the right, 6th Battalion in the centre and 9th Battalion on the left. The first two battalions were to take Gird Trench and Gird Support Trench. On the right, the 28th Australian Division was to attack alongside the 8th Battalion. On the left of the 9th Battalion was an open flank to be neutralised by a heavy barrage laid down by the artillery support.

Roland planned to attack with 'A', 'B' and 'C' Companies in four waves, 30 paces between each wave, with the three companies in line of companies and in columns of platoons. The battalion objectives were the Butte, the quarry in front of it, and parts of Gird Trench and Gird Support. The three attacking companies assembled in Maxwell Trench, which lay some 250 to 300 yards from the Butte. 'D' Company waited further back in The Tail with orders to move forward to Maxwell Trench as soon as the attacking companies vacated. Battalion headquarters was in a dugout in Hexham Road. During the night 4th/5th November the enemy, on two occasions, put down a heavy barrage on Maxwell Trench and The Tail. It poured with rain and a gale force wind added to the misery of the troops as they squelched through the deep mud to the assembly trenches. Standing in muddy water in the trenches and shivering with cold they waited for zero hour. All companies were in position by 6 a.m. on the morning of the 5th. The rain had stopped and the wind had dropped, but it was still bitterly cold. Unknown to the assaulting troops, the Germans were carrying out a relief. The 24th Bavarian Division was being relieved by the 1st Guards Reserve Division, and both were in the trenches opposite or moving in support when the attack began.

At 9.10 a.m., the assault commenced. The heavily loaded troops clambered out of the wet and slippery trenches. The first ones out turned to help those that followed them, grasping hands to pull them out. They formed up in their lines and dragged themselves forward towards the enemy through clinging mud. The pace was agonisingly slow and their objective lay some 250 to 300 yards ahead. They presented a perfect target for the enemy gunfire. Roland wrote in one of his reports to brigade headquarters:

> The German barrage came down at about four minutes after nine-o-clock. There were three barrages, one was a few yards in front of Maxwell Trench, another was on Hexham Road where Battalion Headquarters was situated in a dugout at the entrance to Snag Trench and the third was between Hexham Road and the Flers Line. All were particularly intense.

The Australians and the 8th Battalion were cut to pieces within a short distance of leaving their trenches and the survivors staggered back to the shelter they had just left. The right flanking platoons of the 6th Battalion, under heavy enemy frontal and enfilade fire, suffered a similar fate. The platoons on the left, somewhat protected by the successful advance of the 9th, crossed over two lines of German trenches and established a block in the Gird Line. Roland wrote in his report:

> On the left the 9th DLI met with less opposition and succeeded in gaining all its objectives without suffering heavy casualties…

At 10 a.m. the 9th DLI was disposed as follows: Four Posts were established in the Gird Front Line, the left one being on the Albert–Bapaume Road. There were four Posts in the space between the Butte and Gird front Line. The front edge of the Quarry was strongly held and two Company Headquarters were situated in the Quarry in telephonic communication with Battalion Headquarters. Each of the assaulting platoons had a reserve platoon in Butte Alley, the trench running immediately South of the Butte. Two machine guns were sited in Butte Alley and a 2" Stokes Mortar in the Quarry. Two battalion observers were on the Butte. The Reserve Company of the Battalion was in Maxwell Trench. Eight Bavarian prisoners who had been sent on their way back, together with their escort, had been annihilated by the German artillery fire. The Germans were still holding a dugout on the north east side of the Butte. The parties who should have 'mopped up' the Butte dugouts had either gone forward without completing their work, carried away in the enthusiasm of the assault, or had been shot by German snipers while at their work.

The Germans had now realised the scope of our attack and many of their batteries concentrated their fire on our new positions. Snipers from Warlencourt–Eaucourt were subjecting our men to deadly fire and it was almost impossible for them to move.

The Germans in the dugout on the northeast edge of the Butte have brought a machine gun into position and were worrying us from behind. Many gallant attempts were made throughout the day to capture this dugout without success. All our parties, who tried to rush it were destroyed by the German machine gun fire and the large numbers of snipers in Warlencourt. However a party did succeed in throwing some Mills Grenades into the dugout and this made the Boche more cautious.

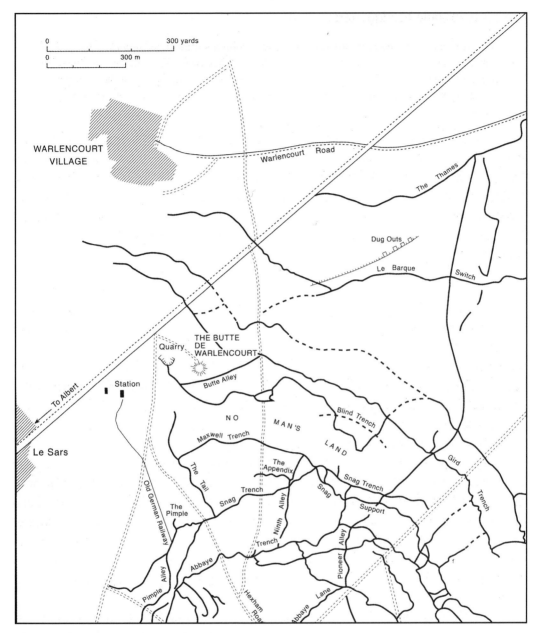

The Butte de Warlencourt, 5th November 1916.

The first German counter-attack was made about noon. It was a half hearted one and was easily stopped. During the afternoon the enemy launched several bombing attacks but these too were repulsed.

The Butte, with the exception of the dugout referred to in the above report, was in British hands. This dugout continued to be a thorn in the British side as it was firing into the flanks and rear of the assaulting troops. Roland again reported to brigade headquarters:

We killed large numbers of the enemy on the Butte and in the Quarry and, owing to heavy fire, could not take so many prisoners as we might otherwise. If another Battalion were attached to me I could probably take the Gird Line from M.17 a 7.7 to M.17 b 3.4. The work on the Communication Trench to Butte is progressing.

From noon till 3 p.m., the position remained the same. Several enemy counter attacks were broken up, but losses were beginning to weaken the battalion's ability to hold these attacks. The Germans had laid a curtain of artillery fire between the battalion's attacking formations and the support troops, making it impossible for the latter to advance. With no reinforcements, the position was becoming desperate. At 3 p.m., the Germans, who were able to reinforce their troops, launched a heavy counter-attack on the Durhams' positions. The fighting was intense, but there is only so much that can be asked of men who had been under severe pressure and against overwhelming odds for so long. Roland reported the action to brigade headquarters:

We have been driven out of Gird Front Line and I believe my Posts there are captured. I have tried to get back but the enemy is in considerable force and is still counter-attacking. It is taking me all my time to hold Butte Alley. Please ask artillery to shell North of Bapaume road in M.10.d to M.11.c as Germans are in considerable force there. Enemy is holding Gird Front Line strongly on my right. In my opinion a strong advance to the right of the Butte would meet with success.

Have a small Post in a shell hole at the N.W. corner of the Butte, but the enemy still has a Post on the Butte on the North side. I am just going to make another effort to capture this Post.

Desperate fighting continued all afternoon. The battalion survivors continued to hold out against intense enemy pressure, and were greatly aided by reinforcements who finally managed to get through. Roland reported:

About 6 p.m. the Germans made a determined counter-attack preceded by a terrific bombardment and were able to get to close quarters. A tough struggle ensued. But our men who had now been reinforced by the Reserve Company and who showed the traditional superiority of the British in hand-to-hand fighting, succeeded in driving out the enemy.

At 7.15 p.m., Roland sent another report:

We are holding Butte Alley from M.17 a 5.5 to M.16 b 9.8. We have a Post on the North side of the Butte at M.17 a 3.7. The enemy still has a Post on the Northern slope of the Butte but I am trying to scupper this. I am now endeavouring to establish a Post in the Gird Front Line at M.17 a 7.6 and another one at M.17 a 3.8. Germans are still attacking and a good deal of hand-to-hand fighting is taking place.

Close fighting with the enemy continued throughout the evening, and the battalion, after so many hours of sustained effort, began to weaken. Roland's commentary to headquarters related the developing events:

At about 11 p.m. Battalions of the Prussians delivered a fresh counter-attack. They came in great force from our front and also worked round both from the flanks. Our men were overwhelmed. Many died fighting. Others were compelled to surrender. It was only a handful of men who found their way back to Maxwell Trench and they were completely exhausted by their great efforts and the strain of fighting.

A day later, on the 7th November, Roland was able to record this final, lethal attack in more detail:

> The enemy counter-attack was delivered from the Gird Line, from the left flank (from the direction of M.16 b 8.9) and from the right flank (from the Gird Line). The Germans, still holding out in the Butte dugout, came out and advanced over the Butte. The enemy advanced throwing bombs. A party of about 20 Germans worked round our left flank and attacked the Quarry in the rear. The enemy was in great strength. This attack was perfectly organised and was pushed in with great energy and determination. The enemy advanced beyond Butte Alley and evidently had intended to capture Maxwell Trench. Our men resisted heroically but after a desperate stand were driven back to Maxwell Trench so that by 1 a.m. on the 6th we were in the same position as on the morning of the 5th prior to the assault.

Another report from Roland followed. It was timed and dated 7 a.m. on the 6th November and forwarded to Brigade on the 7th:

> Operations – We pushed a patrol out to crest north of Maxwell Trench at 5 a.m. but it had to retire owing to heavy fire from left before it had had time to observe anything.
>
> Work Done – NIL
>
> Artillery – Enemy shelled Maxwell Trench heavily throughout the day. At 4 p.m., he directed an intense bombardment on Maxwell Trench and kept this up till 4.30 p.m. – fortunately the barrage was just short. Pimple Alley, Flers Line and Abbaye Lane were kept under heavy shell fire throughout the day.
>
> Miscellaneous – Enemy snipers from direction of Warlencourt made movement across open along the side of Pimple Alley about impossible. Enemy had a sniper on top of the Butte at 10 a.m. but he soon had to clear. Pimple Alley is knee deep in mud almost throughout the length. Herewith some letters taken from the pockets of a badly wounded German in Butte Alley. The lateness of the relief was due to the heavy shelling which compelled the 5th DLI to take cover in Pimple Alley.

The dugout on the northern slope of the Butte must have been quite large as it was estimated that, in addition to the machine gun, it contained about 100 German infantry. The final report from Roland was sent at 12.30 a.m:

> We have been driven out of Butte Alley by a strong counter-attack and 9 DLI and 6 DLI are now in Maxwell Trench. Enemy was in great force and we cannot get back to Butte Alley. All our Posts are captured or driven back.

The casualties suffered by the battalion were considerable: 6 officers were killed, 8 wounded and 3 missing. Of the other ranks, 36 were killed, over 220 wounded and 154 missing. In 151 Brigade, casualties totalled 38 officers and 929 other ranks. Considering that the Butte was thought to have had no real military value, this was a tremendous sacrifice. Throughout the engagement, it is doubtful that Roland would have remained in his headquarters in Hexham Road. Given his personal priority to be close to his attacking companies, it is almost certain that he appeared in the advance headquarters in the Quarry where he could exercise some control over his companies.

At 11 p.m. on the 6th November, the survivors of the 9th Battalion were relieved by the 5th DLI, from 150 Brigade. The battalion moved to the northwest corner of Mametz Wood, which it reached at 3 a.m. on the 7th. Roland wrote a final report on the action and forwarded it to his superiors:

> There were many reasons why the 9th DLI was unable to hold its ground.
>
> The failure of the troops on the right to reach their objective and the fact that the Division on our left was not attacking caused both flanks of the Battalion to be very much in the air. The position to be held was very exposed and the Germans could see all our movements and control their fire accordingly. It was a local attack and the enemy were able to concentrate his guns on a small portion of our line. The ground was a sea of mud and it was almost impossible to consolidate our Posts. The terribly intense German barrages and the difficult nature of the ground prevented reinforcements from being sent up to help 9 DLI. Four hundred yards north of the Butte, the enemy had a steep bank behind which they were able to assemble without being molested. In the hope of being able to exploit success we had arranged for our barrage to be placed just beyond the bank. The terrain was very favourable to a German counter-attack. Beside the splendid observation points in their possession, the ground provided great facilities for the forming up of their troops under cover. At first sight it might appear as if the conditions were reciprocal for we had the Maxwell Trench Ridge, which gave us some cover. But it wasn't really so. The ground between the Flers Line and Hexham Road before getting under the cover of Maxwell Trench Ridge is very exposed and all the ground concealed by the Ridge was intensely shelled by the enemy throughout the day and night…

Roland made sure to praise the bravery of his men, and with characteristic frankness, questioned his superiors of their need to waste the lives of so many for so little:

> It is wonderful, when one considers the difficulties under which our men were working and the fearful fire to which they were exposed, that they held on so long as they did. And it makes you proud to be an Englishman.
>
> On looking back to the attack on the 5th of November, it seems that the results which would have been gained in the event of success were of doubtful value, and would hardly have been worth the loss which we would suffer. It would have been awkward for us to hold the objective, which would have been badly sited for our defence. The possession of the Butte by the Germans was not an asset to them. From our existing trenches we were able to prevent them from using it as an observation point. The Butte itself would have been of little use to us for the purpose of observation.
>
> But the Butte de Warlencourt had become an obsession. Everybody wanted it. It loomed large in the minds of the soldiers in the forward area and they attributed many of their misfortunes to it. The newspaper correspondents talked about 'that Miniature Gibraltar'. So it .

It seems that the attack was one of those tempting and, unfortunately at one period, frequent local operations which are so costly and which are rarely worthwhile.

But perhaps that is only the narrow view of the Regimental Officer.

How his superiors received Roland's report is not known, but there could have been no doubt as to his opinions of the action.

Despite all it had suffered, there was to be little rest for the battalion. The 9th had to provide working parties on the day they came out of the line, in spite of the vicious and demanding fighting which had taken place only a few hours previous. From the 16th to the 30th November, the battalion was at rest in a camp at Millencourt. On the 25th November, an announcement came: Roland was to receive the Victoria Cross for his leadership of the 6th and 9th in the defence of the British line on 1st/2nd October.

In joyous reaction, the men hoisted their young Colonel onto their shoulders and chaired him round the area, refusing to put him down until he agreed to their loud cries of 'Speech, speech!' Roland told them that his award was not merely for himself but for the good work of the whole battalion.

While the battalion was at rest, drafts of 5 officers and 219 other ranks joined to replace losses. Training commenced to integrate the new men and this was continued when the battalion moved to Warloy on the 1st December. As usual, training was intense, but an inter-company football league was started provide some entertainment, and the 9th competed with the other battalions. The battalion stayed in training through to Christmas Day which was celebrated with a meal of pork, which took the place of the traditional turkey. Parcels from home provided extra treats and surprises for Christmas, the Green Diamonds performed and the band played festive tunes. Roland had survived some of the worst fighting of the Somme, and his thoughts at Christmas must have turned to the family at home and his brothers scattered throughout the armed forces.

Chapter 8

1917

If Roland was thinking of the family at Christmas 1916, it would have been appropriate for he was not alone on the Somme. James rejoined his battalion – the 18th DLI – on the Somme front in mid-October 1916. In January and February 1917, the battalion was in the Hebuterne Sector of the Somme front. On the 21st February, it moved to Sailly and on the 25th of the month occupied trenches in front of Gommecourt. During the following weeks, the Germans were withdrawing from their positions and moving back into new and powerful trench systems, which became known as the Hindenburg Line. Their rearguards put up a stout resistance. On the 3rd March the 18th Battalion pressed forward in an attempt to take a German strongpoint known as Garde Stellung. The Germans occupied this position in force and fiercely repelled the battalion's attempts to break in. The Durhams were held up by strong wire and trench blocks and the attacking companies were withdrawn so that an artillery barrage could be put down on the enemy lines. The battalion history states:

> On cessation of the bombardment the Companies which had gradually been creeping up dashed in at once overpowering the garrison, taking 35 prisoners and two machine guns, Second Lieutenants H.E. Hitchen M.M., and J.B. Bradford showing fine leadership.

The attack was successful, and the strongpoint fell to this assault.

Word of James's success reached the rest of the family. In a letter to sister Amy dated 23rd March 1917, George Bradford wrote:

> Jimmy has been doing very well and I trust a grateful country may give him a decoration. I think he strongly deserves it for his all round ability and most important of all, tenacity, or in the homely expression but unladylike phrase "guts".

This letter also reveals that their mother was in poor health:

> Poor mother has had a bad time lately with heart weakness and fainting fits. Nancy [James's wife] is looking after her.

As George hoped, James was awarded a medal. The *London Gazette* of the 17th April 1917 contained a citation for the award of the Military Cross to James:

> For conspicuous gallantry and devotion to duty. He gallantly led his men into the enemy trench, capturing many prisoners and two machine guns. He himself killed three of the enemy. Later, he succeeded in repelling a determined enemy counter-attack.

In a letter to their mother on the 26th April 1917, George commented on the family's successes:

> I am awfully proud and pleased that your third warrior J.B.B. has been given the M.C. *The Times* newspaper gave a short description of his hat-trick achievement, of bowling 3 over…In addressing the envelope I feel inclined to put Mrs. Bradford V.C., D.S.O., M.C. [VC for Roland; DSO for Thomas and MC for James].

His letter also addresses her health:

> I hope you are getting stronger although of course it must be gradual as you were run down and needed a good rest. Many thanks for your and Amy's birthday wishes [George turned 30 on 23rd April]. I am glad that Amy did well at school, she must have grown into a fine big girl by now (perhaps I should have said, 'a finer than ever'). All is going excellently with us and we have never been more ready for the grand coup. I hope you get some fine summer weather soon, that will do you more good than anything else.

In this state of poor health, mother was to face the first tragic death of one of her sons.

On the 25th March, James and the 18th Battalion were at Bethune. For the next few weeks, the battalion moved from one place to another, usually in reserve and carrying out many hard and humdrum tasks needed to support comrades in the front line. James wrote to Amy in good humour on the 22nd April, just three weeks before his death:

> Dear Ginger,
>
> Many happy returns of the day, thank you for your letters and the tie, it is top-hole one. You will be sorry you are going back to school again. So the tortoise has come alive again, well keep an eye on it and see it does not chase the hens about, it will keep mother busy feeding it again. I think we should put it down owing to the present food restrictions.

On the night of the 2nd/3rd May, James's battalion was in reserve to the 15th, 16th and 18th Battalions of the West Yorkshire Regiment, who had been ordered to attack Gavrelle. The attack started at 4.30 a.m. on the 3rd May. The assaulting battalions ran into a heavy German artillery bombardment, which was followed by strong infantry counter-attacks from the enemy. Although James is not mentioned by name in any of the reports on the action, he would have been involved with the rest of the Durhams. The battalion was relieved on the night of the 4th–5th May, but returned to the front line east of Gavrelle on the 7th. Heavy enemy artillery barrages continued to fall on the front positions. On the night of the 10th–11th May, the battalion was relieved once more, but not before the enemy guns had inflicted their nightly share of casualties.

On this night in the trenches, James Bradford received gunshot wounds to his left shoulder and left thigh while the relief was taking place. He could have first been attended at the Regimental Aid Post in the trenches, and moved as soon as possible to a Casualty Clearing Post some distance behind the front line. We do not know what treatment or care he received, but doubtless he would have lost a great quantity of blood. Whatever could have been done for him was to no end, and he died at the Clearing Post on the 14th May. On the 17th, Mrs. Bradford received the dreaded telegram from Buckingham Palace:

> The King and Queen deeply regret the loss you and the army have sustained by the death of your son in the service of his country. Their Majesties truly sympathise with you in your sorrow.

The wounds James suffered did not appear to have been to any vital part of his body and he should have been expected to survive. Certainly his wife Nancy was very unhappy with the treatment he received and she criticised his doctors in a letter to her husband's batman. The letter, written from Grange House, Darlington, was dated 11th June 1917, and tells a great deal about how a young wife dealt with the news:

> Dear Mr. Alderson,
>
> Thank you for your kind letter. I know how you feel about his death. It seems so hard that he should be taken when he could have done so much good in the world.
>
> I am so pleased to hear that you are expecting leave shortly. I am enclosing you a postcard which you could perhaps send me when you get home letting me know which day you will come to Darlington and I will come over to see you. I am at present in a Harrowgate Nursing Home as I have been ill ever since I had the terrible news and I do not on any account want to miss you, so if you could send me the postcard I should be obliged. I am getting Mr. Bradford's kit home by degrees.
>
> Mr. Dugdale very kindly went to see me at home last week and I was most sorry to miss him, it would have been so nice to have heard something about my husband.
>
> I must thank you for asking Sergt. Major Curry to write me details about my husband, I had a very kind letter from him and it was a comfort to hear something definite. I do feel that those people in the hospital have simply thrown his life away by giving him the operation when he was not strong enough to stand it, if only they had waited I think everything would have been well for him.
>
> Hoping you are well and that I shall see you soon, and again many thanks for your kind sympathy.

Thomas wrote to his mother on the 21st May, from Femoy in Ireland where he was stationed:

> You will know that poor old Jimmie has gone out, it is a very sad business, he was a great fellow.
>
> I think Kipling's words are more true of him than most of us. 'He scarce had need to doff his pride or slough the dross of earth. E'en as he trod that day to God, so he walked from his birth. In humbleness and honesty and honour and clean mirth.'
>
> There is little consolation to be got except that his life has been quite happy and he went out of it a great fellow and we must remember that he would want us to meet this blow with a firm face and try to do the extras amount of good in this world that he himself have done had he been spared.

I am writing to Nancy.

Hoping you are getting better. With love

On the same day Roland wrote to Nancy:

It was very kind and thoughtful of you to send me the telegram containing the sad news about poor Jimmy's death. I can understand how much you feel the loss and you have my deepest sympathy. But keep a brave heart, and think of the noble and gallant way in which he fought for our righteous cause; and remember that one day we shall all meet again and will attain a happiness far greater than that we are now capable of conceiving. How thankful I feel that he and I met last April. I shall never forget the true manly look in his dear eyes when we parted from each other. May God help you, as he is helping me to bear up under your grief.

It was most kind of you to accompany mother to London. I hope you are keeping well. Will you please give my love to Mrs. Wall and Mrs. Fry.

I have written to Jimmy's battalion to find out where he is buried and I hope soon to be able to visit the grave. I send you my best wishes…

Whether or not he got the chance to visit James's grave in the Duisans British Military Cemetery, near Arras, is not known. Roland certainly visited his mother and Nancy in June while he was home on leave to collect his VC.

George also wrote to comfort Nancy from HMS Orion on the 23rd May:

I am awfully sorry and feel deeply for you. We can both be absolutely certain that poor old Jimmie died a hero's death and met it like the hero he was and is. Words fail me to say more but I think you will know what I feel.

Thank you for looking after mother, it must have been trying for you.

George again wrote to sister Amy on the 26th May:

Thank you for your letter of the 10th May. I suppose you have heard the sad news of poor old Sling, no matter; he was a hero and we can be certain faced his end like the fine large hearted fellow he always was. Poor Nancy will be cut up about it…

From all the letters and shared consolation, we get a sense of the Bradfords rallying together in grief. We can only guess at the magnitude of the loss to the family. The brothers, with their high sense of duty, kept tight control of their emotions, which had been a central part of the family teaching throughout their young years. Instead, their concern turned toward their mother's health. This is shown in George's letter to Amy:

You must try and buck mother up all you can as you will realise she has done a lot for us and at present leads a very lonely life.

In addition to the family tributes, Nancy received a letter from Capt. Chappell, the Chaplain of the 18th Battalion, dated 24th May:

I hardly know what to write to you. One always feels, of course, that in a home where a soldier falls, there is deep sorrow. But, somehow or other, knowing your husband so well, I feel that your grief must be intense to a degree. I write chiefly to try to give you comfort on this point – that your husband always live a life very near to the Saviour. He was always regular in his communion and carried the strength he received at the altar in all his duties. He was a truly magnificent man and I can't put it into words how deeply his loss is felt by all ranks…I remember when he led the raid a few months ago how he brought his men a few hours before to commend themselves to their maker…

George's concern for his mother's condition continued, as seen in a letter to his sister dated 1st July 1917:

You are right about the canoe, the stern is the place to steer from – only great men like me can do it from forward. I suppose you like David Copperfield. Dombey and Son is one of my favourites. Here is a crest, very few have come my way lately but I shall remember you want them. You should give mother an optimistic letter from time-to-time. She has been much shaken by her illness and Jimmy.

His letter concludes in an optimistic, light-hearted fashion:

Weather here glorious, winning the war, in fact everything going splendidly. No aches, no pains, a pleasure to be alive.

As referred to in his letter, George was sending Amy the crests of warships, which she was obviously collecting. He sent another with an undated letter:

…The enclosed is a somewhat fantastic crest. The animal is actually a flea, it strikes one as rather heavily misplaced wit…Good luck to you at school, keep the Bradford name like that of Bayard, 'chevalier sans peur' – possibly mis-quoted but conveys the right idea.

I think the war is going well and the prospects excellent, don't allow anyone with a long face to say otherwise. That is my personal propaganda and I am certain it is right.

On a personal level, things were certainly going well for George. In a letter dated 5th August 1917, George informed Amy of his promotion:

Moi, I am a Lieutenant Commander having completed 8 years as Lieutenant and, as the designing mothers of Plymouth would say, 'He gets another shilling a day now'.

The *Daily Mail* says that the Durhams have enhanced their fighting reputation in the recent offensive. I hope the Colonel [Roland] has done well.

Lieutenant George Bradford, 1918.

As George hoped, Roland was doing very well. In 1917, Roland was to show that he was indeed a military commander of great skill, but as with James, the year would end with his untimely death.

The year 1917 started for Roland much as it had ended. On the 31st December 1916 his 9th Battalion moved again into the front line trenches of the Somme at Factory Corner. Continued rain and snow showers had left the trenches in a terrible condition. For the whole of January 1917, the battalion was in the line or in support, until it moved to Ribemont at the end of the month. With the muddy, cold conditions, it was perhaps a relief to Roland that there was no fighting during January except for short periods of artillery shellfire, sniping and patrolling. Roland spent most of each day in the trenches talking to his officers and men and overseeing arrangements for their safety and comfort, and organising and leading training and fitness activities. It was during one of his tours on the 16th January that he was wounded slightly, along with the Medical Officer, Capt. J.A.C. Scott (RAMC). Both remained on duty. On the 4th February, Roland presented gold medals to the winning team of the battalion football league, which was Headquarter Company, and silver medals to 'D' Company, the runners up. On the 12th of the month, the battalion marched to Foucaucourt, where the 50th Division had relieved the 35th and 36th French Infantry Divisions. More training followed and, ensuring that there was a balance between work and play, an inter-platoon football knockout competition was started. On the 16th, a comic costume parade caused a great deal of amusement.

On the night of the 23rd/24th February, the battalion was back in the front line in the Berny sector. On the 27th, Roland left to attend a brief senior officers course and Maj. Crouch assumed command. On the 2nd March, the battalion moved to Mericourt-sur-Somme. This was a new training area, and Roland immediately ordered and supervised the building of first-class training area with bombing pits, a rifle range and an assault course. With this facility, he could start putting into operation the lessons he had learned in the Somme battles. He had been thinking for some time about how to attack across no man's land without the huge losses of former battles. The War Diary entry of the 15th March mentions that training on that day focused on new attack and bombing formations. Roland had long preached that the training methods of pre-war days that emphasised fire and movement were just as important in this war as formerly. While the War Diary does not detail the actual methods now being taught (or retaught!), training certainly included dashes across no man's land, using the ground cover provided by shell holes, and aided by bombers in close proximity ready to attack any machine gun nest that might hamper progress and cause enormous casualties. Fluidity of movement and mutual support were emphasised. The men were trained to fire their rifles and even Lewis guns from the hip, enabling them to move more quickly. How well these lessons were learned became apparent in later battles.

On the 28th March, the battalion was inspected by Lt. Gen. Sir W.P. Pulteney,

GOC III Army Corps. The War Diary entry records his impressions:

> He thanked the officers, NCOs and men of the 151 Infantry Brigade for the good work they had done on the Somme while under his command and hoped they would be as successful in the XVIII Corps, to which they were going, as they had been in III Corps. After wishing all good luck, the Brigade marched past in Column of Route.

Roland led this parade at the head of his marching men, on his grey charger as always.

Over the next fortnight, the battalion gradually moved towards Arras, reaching Beaurains and moving into the reserve line on the 11th April. The Battle of Arras had started two days previously. The Germans were now occupying their formidable Hindenburg Line.

On the night of the 13th April, the 9th Battalion relieved the 10th Battalion DLI in the line. The 10th was commanded by Col. H.H.S. Morant, who had been one of Roland's commanding officers when Roland was in the 2nd Battalion. Col. Morant wrote:

> His [Roland's] Battalion came up to relieve mine after the first two days of the Battle of Arras. It was an awful night, dark as pitch, with a blizzard raging. He arrived at my dugout about midnight. After greeting me most respectfully, though we were of similar rank, and after a brief and modest account of his recent doings in the war in answer to my enquiries, he asked me to excuse him whilst he issued orders to his Second-in-Command, Quartermaster and Transport Officer. The way he gave these orders impressed me greatly. Though he had come up in the dark and in a blizzard to a perfectly strange locality, he had noticed positions for cookers, transport lines and everything and everyone; and proceeded to give clear and brief but comprehensive orders to each one. This lad, who barely five years previously had been attached to me for preliminary training was now, unconsciously no doubt, giving me a lesson as to how things ought to be done.

The plan of attack for the 14th April was that the 56th Division would attempt to capture Chérisy and the 50th Division would advance alongside to protect its left flank. The latter division would then form a defensive line on the left flank, facing northwards and following the high ground with its left on Wancourt Tower. The plan for the battalions of 151 Brigade was for 9 DLI to remain stationary, and by so doing to protect against any enemy counter-attack from Guemappes, which was still held by the Germans. The 6th Battalion DLI attacked in line with the 56th Division. It was followed by the 8th Battalion. Under intense harassing fire from the direction of Guemappes, both battalions suffered heavy casualties and became intermingled with units from the 56th Division. By evening three companies of 8 DLI were in position on the left of the 6th Battalion, just west of Wancourt Tower. One and one-half companies of the 9th Battalion held the ground with their right on the ruined Tower and facing northeast. The remaining two and one-half companies were just east of the River Cojeul. Roland's report gives a full account of his battalion's involvement:

At 9 .m. on the 13th April, I sent forward two strong patrols to establish themselves on the ridge near Wancourt Tower. These patrols met with considerable opposition but by 12 noon one Post was established on the left of the Tower at N.24 d.2.2 and another in the road at N.24 d. 1.1/2.

At about 2.30 p.m., an attempt was made but without success to drive enemy from position near N.30 b 1.9 where there was very active machine gun fire. We then occupied the house at N.24 d. 1/2 and brought rifle fire to bear on enemy position from there. The house was soon rendered untenable by shellfire. At about 3 p.m., enemy intensely shelled our Post in the road and we had to withdraw lower down the road.

At dusk on the 13th, Posts were pushed forward close to the Tower. At 10 p.m., the enemy blew up the Tower. On the night of the 13th/14th, a trench was dug twenty yards from the Tower from N.30 b.0.9 to N.24 d 1.1/2. The enemy undoubtedly intended to counter-attack the position but was prevented from so doing by the activity of our patrols. Our position was intensely shelled on the 14th but as the men had dug an excellent trench few casualties were suffered.

Until the battalion moved out of the line on the 15th April, it was subjected to continuous machine gun fire, to which it replied with Lewis guns and machine guns, and succeeded in causing the enemy to cease fire. On the 15th it moved to Ronville Caves. Here it was safe from enemy shelling, but the caves were extremely damp and cold and an unpleasant foggy atmosphere affected the men's breathing. Roland's report on the actions to date included his assessment of the lessons learnt:

Lessons: As stated above before dawn on the 13th April, our patrols found that there was no enemy within 500yds of our line. Our relief was completed too late to enable us to push forward then. The enemy must have moved back towards our line at dawn and this shows us the importance of the principle, 'advance your line while ye may'.

The old maxims were burnt into our souls:

1. Consolidate with all possible energy so as to provide protection from shellfire.

2. Protect yourself against counter-attack by energetic patrolling.

3. When moving up to dig trenches be quiet and stop all jangling equipment and tools.

The battalion remained in the caves until the 23rd April. On this day they left Ronville at 7 a.m. and marched to a sector known as 'The Harp', named for the elaborate wire defences the Germans had built to protect it. The area was now in British hands, and the battalion rested here until ordered to proceed to Nepal Trench to help 150 Brigade repel a counter-attack. Before the 9th got moving, the orders had changed and instead it was to move into the front line to recapture lost trenches, and was to be ready to attack at 6 p.m.. Roland's report to Brig. Gen. Cameron describes how this was achieved:

At 4 p.m. the Battalion moved in artillery formation to the Bank in N24 a & b and then formed up for assault behind our line in N 24 b – the line which we had dug on night of 14th/15th April. Two companies were leading, each with three platoons in first wave and one in Company Reserve. The two remaining companies were in support – one on the right and one on the left, both to follow at 100yds distance from last line of company in front of them. At 6 p.m. the barrage came down about 20yds in front of our trench and remained there for 10 minutes. This caused great anxiety and one or two casualties were suffered. At 6.10 p.m. the barrage moved forward and we advanced close up to it. After an advance of about 200yds an enemy machine gun on the railway opened fire. Our right company fired several rifle grenades at this gun and the team then surrendered. About 400yds from our original trench the German line was encountered very strongly held and with several machine guns in position. From this point our advance was continued in section rushes and the supporting companies, which were in artillery formation, were compelled to extend. Accurate rifle and Lewis Gun fire were kept up on the enemy trench and the Rifle Grenadiers, when they had rushed forward within range, opened an effective fire on the enemy trench. The left company which did not meet with so much opposition as the right company, penetrated the enemy trench and delivered a bombing attack on the Germans. Directly the latter perceived that we were on their flank, they surrendered. They were escorted to the Aid Post by several of our slightly wounded men.

Two of our machine guns (150 M.G. Company) were left at this trench to give protection against counter-attack and also a party of 1 NCO and about ten men as moppers up. The advance continued without great opposition for another 300yds, when several enemy machine guns opened heavy fire at close range on to us. A short tussle took place in which our sections employed the principle of "mutual support" most effectively and the teams of six enemy guns were destroyed or captured. The enemy was now in a panic and we were able to advance to the objective troubled only by long-range machine gun fire from about St. Rohart Factory. We poured fire into the retreating Germans and inflicted heavy casualties on them.

The position was consolidated with all speed and Lewis Gun Posts were established about 300yds in advance of our line. Our flanks, which were both exposed, were drawn back...Our patrols were active during the night and took some prisoners. Evidently, the enemy had intended to make a counter-attack but our patrols and advanced posts stopped him carrying it out...Rations and stores on the nights 23rd/24th and 24th/25th, were carried up to front line on pack ponies.

As usual with so many of Roland's reports to army command, he followed with the lessons learnt:

This attack was an open attack and rifles and Lewis Guns were used to full advantage for covering fire.

The vulnerability of a flank was clearly demonstrated. In the advance, as described in my narrative, our line was held up. Those held up kept up an effective fire with their rifles and Lewis Guns, the rifle bombers worked forward till within range and opened fire, while the company on the left, worked round the enemy's flank. So, soon as the enemy realised his flank was gone, he surrendered.

Rifles were fired from the hip with good effect whilst on the move. The Lewis Gun was, in one instance, fired effectively from the shoulder. When we had gained the objective we had about 50 rounds of small arms ammunition per man left. There were a large number of enemy "tatiemasher" bombs lying about and these were collected and placed ready for use. So were the German rifles and small arms ammunition. Very small escorts were provided for prisoners and these were mainly slightly wounded men.

Our barrage, though too slow was very effective and our men kept right up to it the whole time. The great power of the Lewis Gun was forcibly demonstrated.

Maj. Crouch, Second in Command commented:

> By its quick delivery, led by the Colonel in the first wave, it outflanked the enemy who immediately surrendered. This action was one of the most successful carried out by us. Having regard for the results obtained, casualties were extremely small. The line was re-established and remained firmly in our hands. We captured over 300 prisoners, two large howitzers, which the enemy had destroyed, and many machine guns, 13 of which were serviceable…The enemy dead were strewn about the area.

> This action would have gladdened the heart of the stoutest martinet, the value of 'training, training, training' being forced home to the most casual observer. The men under their section, platoon or company commanders, worked as though on an ordinary practice attack.

The 6th and 8th Battalions of the brigade had also acquitted themselves well in this action. Brig. Cameron wrote the following in a report dated the 28th April 1917:

> I hope and trust that the Brigade knows well already how warmly I congratulate all Units on their very successful encounter with the enemy.

> The recent operation should have succeeded in knitting together, more firmly than ever, the Brigade inside our Division and the Units inside our Brigade. Can we now say, in the generous words of Nelson, our splendid national hero, 'We are in truth a band of brothers' – If so, then no horde of Bosches can stand against us.

Roland's training methods were now paying dividends. Firing their weapons as they advanced, rifle grenadiers blasting grenades into machine gun positions, bombers working on the flanks and sections of men rushing forward rather than attacking in lines were methods developed and drilled in training. It is understandable that, following this action, the 9th Battalion was earmarked to form part of 18 Corps de Chasse, whose job was to quickly follow any inroads made on enemy positions by attacking infantry, and to continue the momentum of the attack by not allowing the enemy to reform and consolidate. The creation of the 18 Corps de Chasse, however, was somewhat premature as conditions were not yet appropriate to warrant its use. The battalion reverted to its original role as part of 151 Brigade on the 22nd May.

The British Army was keen to build upon the experiences of commanding officers, recording and passing along their advice and lessons. Following the actions outlined above, on the 28th April Brig. Gen. Cameron posed the following questions to his battalion commanders. These are a selection of Roland's replies, which the Brig. Gen. forwarded to Brigade two days later:

> Question: Is not the pre-war method of attack the method we want to practice? Is it not a mistake to rely on the Artillery barrage alone to overcome all resistance?

> Reply: The pre war method of attack is, in my opinion, the only method which we should practice. The old principle of "mutual support" – fire and movement – is the only method of gaining success. The artillery barrage is of immense importance in

overcoming enemy resistance but we should not rely upon it entirely. The weapons at our disposal are sufficient to enable us to overcome all local resistance.

Question: Do we make too much or too little of the Rifle Grenade? Is the number we carry – 40 per Platoon – about the correct number?

Reply: I consider that adequate use is made of the rifle grenade. It is an invaluable weapon for breaking down enemy resistance. The present number 40 per Platoon, is just what is necessary.

Question: Do we make too much or too little of the Hand Grenade? Is the number we carry – 40 per Platoon – about the correct number?

Reply: Too much. The value of the hand grenade is not now nearly so great as in trench fighting. A few should be carried for special occasions. Twenty per Platoon is, in my opinion a suitable number. Full use should always be made of the German stick grenades found in captured trenches.

Question: Do our men use their rifles and bayonets as much as they ought?

Reply: Yes. The wonderful power of the rifle and bayonet cannot be too strongly realised.

Question: It has been suggested that there should be some definite understanding about the collection of prisoners during an attack, as numbers get very quickly reduced if every man who captures a Bosche immediately walks him back. What are your views?

Reply: This is an important point. It should be definitely laid down that no escort shall exceed 10% and slightly wounded men should be used as far as possible. Men must be told that they are not to move back with prisoners unless they are ordered to do so.

In a letter to Brig. Gen. Cameron dated the 3rd May 1917, Roland added one further point to those outlined above:

In the advance, Sections should rush forward from one shell hole to another whenever possible. We did this with great benefit. It is the old principle, to which we attached so much importance before the war in the training of Section Commanders, 'Select your next position before you advance and point out this position to your Section'. A shell hole gives good cover and is very suitable for firing from.

On the 27th April, the battalion moved to Warluzel, which lies between Arras and Doulens, for a period of rest, re-equipping and training. In the usual style of Roland, training was arduous but concerts and sport programmes balanced work and relaxation. The battalion War Diary entry of the 9th May relates:

Range – Field firing scheme. All advanced as in a trench attack. First line firing from the hip. When held up Rifle Grenades used. Counter-attack organised. Machine guns gave overhead fire. Dinner served on the range at Lucheux. Back in billets 9 p.m. All enjoyed day's outing.

It is probably during this period of rest that the hymn 'Abide with Me' was first sung in the regiment. Col. W.D.B. Thompson DSO, MC, wrote in November 1973:

The foundation of the Durham Light Infantry Regimental Hymn 'Abide With Me' was consequent of the leadership of one, Roland Boys Bradford, VC, MC.

During 1917 the 9th Battalion Durham Light Infantry (151 Infantry Brigade 50th Northumbrian Division) were, after the Battle of Arras, in reserve near Vimy Ridge when, in the early evening, a Battalion order came round stating the Battalion would parade in clean fatigue at Battalion H.Q.

Duly assembled and with the Battalion Band also on parade R.B.B. came out of the H.Q. marquee and said:

'My friends, I believe in God and I want you all to sing the hymn the Band will play; not only now but every night wherever you are, in the trenches, reserve line or billets.'

The Band struck up and 'Abide With Me' was sung.

At the end the companies marched back to their respective areas.

'Abide with Me' summed up Roland's personal feelings about the nature of the war in which the British were engaged, and he viewed it as a source of comfort and confirmation that God was on their side. The adoption the hymn for the 9th DLI was important for Roland. In addition to calling the company together especially to introduce it, he made it part of the initiation of new members. A speech made to new drafts in the summer of 1917 explains the depth of feeling he had for 'Abide with Me' as well as his pride in the entire battalion:

Comrades, I want to welcome you all to the 9th Durham Light Infantry. Most of you will have heard something of our battalion. It has a great reputation. That reputation is not built by one or two flash-in-the-pan incidents. It has been built up by the hard, honest work and soldierly conduct of the men at all times, and by their skill and pluck in action during a period of over two years Active Service.

Our battalion is universally respected and envied. So you see a great responsibility rests with you. You have got to help us to maintain and even increase our present efficiency.

You must always do the best work of which you are capable, try hard and conscientiously to keep yourself fit, happy and efficient. Make yourselves masters of your own particularly job as soldiers; do your duty willingly and thoroughly.

The call of duty is a sacred one. We must do our duty, not merely to gain praise and advancement thereby, but because it is our duty to ourselves, our comrades, our battalion, our families, our country, our King and to the God who made us, and who will help us in our work.

You will find that you will be happy in this battalion. You will find some splendid friends. Your officers and non-commissioned officers are men who realise that they are made of the same clay as you, and are in sympathy with your difficulties and will do all they can to look after your interests. They know their job and will lead you well at all times.

We are all working for the same purpose, the complete defeat of the enemy, and we must work together, each for each, and all for each.

On behalf of all the gallant lads whom I have the honour to command, I welcome you to our midst. You are now of us, and will work with us and for us.

My friends I am going to arrange for the band to play one verse of the hymn 'Abide With Me'. I would like all of you to join in the words. It should mean more to you than the signing of a well-known hymn. 'Abide With Me' should be no mere catchphrase with us.

It means that we realise that there is Someone who really abides with us and who will help us to help ourselves. Someone who is with us in all our sorrows and hardships, and every man in the world has their fare share of that.

We soldiers should find great comfort in that fact, however much our comrades and those about us may overlook our work, there is Someone who sees and appreciates it. He is with us, I say, just as our friends Sergeant Caldwell, Corporal Guy and Private Holley are now serving with Him.

Sgt. Caldwell DCM, MM and Cpl. Guy MM were killed on the 14th June 1917. Pte. Holley was killed on the following day.

Also in the summer, Roland returned briefly to England to collect his VC. On the 28th May 1917 he wrote of the impending trip and other

Roland Bradford in Civilian Dress, 1917.

events to Maj. Crouch who was on leave:

I hope that you arrived safely and found Mrs. Crouch and family in good health.

We are still resting not far from our last place. Our billets are very good and so is the training area. I was very pleased to see that you were Mentioned in Despatches. The Doc. has been awarded the Croix de Guerre and a Bar to his Military Cross. Jolley, Hall, Wylie and W.D.B. Thompson have been awarded the Military Cross. Bowdery has been granted a Bar to his. Sgt. Caldwell has the D.C.M.

The Green Diamonds gave a very good concert last night in a big barn at one of our billets.

You will be surprised to know that I proceed to England tomorrow to attend the investiture on Saturday. I return to France on Monday June 4th – or on the 5th. I made a hard fight to get out of it. But the General said he, 'Could not disobey a direct order from the King'. Catheral will command during my absence with Bowdery ready to take command on my Brigade Field Days should there be any.

We expect to be in our present position for another fortnight. The men are all very fit now. Forgive me for not writing more now but I am just off to catch my train. I will write you again in a day or two. Au Revoir and with best wishes.

Yours ever,

Roland Bradford.

P.S. Remember don't be nervous about getting back on any particular day. A week or so will not be noticed by anyone.

On the 2nd June 1917, Roland attended Hyde Park, London for the investiture by King George V. During this leave he visited home in Darlington, and no doubt was delighted to see his mother and James's wife Nancy. The Mayor wanted to arrange a public welcome, but Roland refused to agree to one and threatened to get back onto the first train to London if this proposal went ahead. He did not like the thought of 'pomp and ceremony' and felt that any public appreciation should wait till after the war had been won.

Rest and training continued at Warluzel, Monchy-au-Bois, St Amand, Hénin-sur-Cojeul and Boisleux-au-Mont until the 3rd July. At 9 p.m. on this day, the battalion moved into the line opposite Vis-en-Artois, the left sub-sector of the 50th Division's positions. For some time, Roland had insisted on communication trenches being dug wide enough to allow ponies to bring rations and supplies up to battalion headquarters, so protecting carrying parties and saving them much labour. The battalion spent 14 days straight in the line experiencing quite heavy enemy artillery fire and suffering a number of casualties, but no infantry engagements took place. Nights were spent patrolling no man's land. Out of the line, the 9th furnished working parties, though whenever possible concerts and recreational activities were organised. This was the sequence of events until early September 1917.

This somewhat quiet time enabled Roland to engage in other pursuits. He wrote to his mother on the 26th August:

I hope you are keeping well.

You will find a great change in the garden. I can imagine how glorious everything is looking. Events are moving very favourably for us over here. The weather has been constantly fine for many days. I am able to obtain fresh fruit – apples, pears and grapes – everyday from my present locality. Yesterday I competed in a tent pegging competition – but did not win.

I am starting a Shakespeare Reading Society in my Battalion and have written to Baileys for copies of Julius Caesar and Othello. The men are extremely fond of Shakespeare's Works. Baby would enjoy her stay in Ireland. I heard from Georgie last week. Please remember me to the Markhams and to Mrs. Hall and Mrs. J.B. [brother James's wife], if you see them.

With best love and hoping you are looking after yourself and taking things easy.

I am,

Your affectionate Son,

Roland Bradford

She must have been warmed to hear that the love of literature she worked to install in Roland was now being passed to those he served with. Unfortunately, the reading group would have to shortly take a back seat. An entry in the battalion

War Diary on the 6th September 1917 warns of a forthcoming engagement:

> Conference about a forth-coming raid in the morning…Practice in the attack over replica trenches during the afternoon.

The raid was to take place on Narrow Trench, in front of the village of Chérisy, on the 15th September. The planning and execution of the raid would show the qualities of leadership and tactics that came to be associated with Roland. In the raid, innovative methods of training he had installed in his battalion over the previous year would result in a success that was later held up by the British Army as a model for future raids.

The battalion War Diary also carried the following entry for the 11th September:

> The Battalion carried out a practice attack over replica trenches with the Army, Corps, Divisional and Brigade Commanders watching.

When Narrow Trench was dug by the Germans, it was originally well behind the front line. As such, it had not been built with traverses and bays that a front-line trench would normally have. Instead, it was completely straight, which seemed to indicate that its original purpose may have been for communication or to ease the lateral movement of reinforcements to the front line. Due to the British advance, it was now in the German front line and faced the battalion's positions. Heavy shelling and mortaring of this straight trench would have made it impossible for the enemy to hold without serious casualties, and it could be anticipated that the Germans would not have put up much resistance against a serious attack. Yet at the time, it appeared that the Germans were intending to hold the trench. It was occupied by units of the 2/76th Reserve Infantry Regiment 17th Reserve Division, many of whose number came from the Hamburg area of Germany.

If the enemy could have been blasted out of Narrow Trench by heavy artillery fire, why then was a raid necessary, and why did high-ranking senior officers observe preparations and training on the 11th September? It is possible, in the light of subsequent events, that this was an opportunity to see the young battalion commander Roland Bradford displaying the talents he was known to possess, and that he was being watched in order to ascertain his readiness for promotion.

The plan for the raid included an artillery fire programme that was impressive by any standards. The 50th Division's mortars – comprising 2-inch, 3-inch medium and 9.45-inch heavy mortars – began an intensive programme to cut the enemy's wire defences in front of Narrow Trench. This commenced on the 3rd September, 12 days before the raid was carried out. Four days later, the divisional artillery commenced a general bombardment of the Chérisy area. In order to confuse the Germans of British intentions, the bombardment covered a wider area than that which it was intended to raid. Most shells fell in the area west of Chérisy. Aerial observation seemed to indicate that the Germans were strengthening Narrow Trench. A machine gun post was spotted in a sap opposite the position where 'A' Company of the battalion would advance from their trenches. As the day of the raid approached, the artillery bombardment switched to more specific targets. On the 11th September, the divisional artillery opened fire on Narrow Trench itself, while 2-inch mortars continued to cut the wire in front of the trench. The VI Corps artillery now joined in, bombarding both Narrow and Night Trenches. As the day of the raid approached, the artillery of 12th and 16th Divisions brought enfilade fire down on Narrow Trench. A spotter aircraft would follow the advancing infantry and photograph their progress from the air.

The infantry plan, drawn up by Roland, was equally impressive. The raid would be carried out by three companies of the 9th Battalion. After a short period following their attack, a company of the 8th Battalion DLI would attack Narrow Trench with the objective of catching the Germans off guard as they cleared up and attended to their dead and wounded, thus inflicting further loss on the enemy. The objective of both raids was to identify the enemy units holding Narrow Trench, ascertain their morale, strength and quality, and to kill as many as possible. Dugouts and strong points were to be destroyed by explosives. 'A', 'B' and 'C' Companies of the 9th and 'C' Company of the 8th Battalion (under Capt. B.M. Williams) trained over replica trenches for several days until the roles were absolutely clear to each officer and other rank taking part. Eight stretcher-bearers from other battalions in the brigade were attached to the raiders. On the northern and southern flanks of the raiders, dummy troops were to be placed out in no man's land, with the intention of deceiving the enemy and attracting the fire from his artillery away from the actual attackers. A dummy tank, erected by the 7th Field Company Royal Engineers, was placed in front of the trenches as part of this deception. Once the attack got underway, British artillery would fire smoke to cover the enemy distress flares that would certainly be sent up to call their own artillery and support troops. To further confuse the enemy, officers with Verey pistols were to be placed along the front-line trenches to fire flares to duplicate those of the enemy. By so doing, it was hoped that the enemy artillery would be attracted to areas beyond the attack. Both flanks of the raiders would be protected by Lewis Guns, two rifle bombers and two snipers.

When the training was completed every officer and other rank in the attacking companies knew his task and exactly what was expected of him. On the 14th September, 'A', 'B' and 'C' Companies and Roland with battalion headquarters moved into the line. The weather was cold and there were showers of rain. The companies had relieved the 8th Battalion, though the latter continued to provide patrols during the night 14th/15th September. A patrol of the 9th went with them to reconnoitre the ground over which the advance would be made and, on its return to the line, it cut gaps in the wire to allow access to no man's land. The artillery and mortars continued to blast the enemy wire and trenches to ensure that he did not venture out to repair the damage. All was ready for the raid to start on the 15th September.

The weather on the morning of the 15th was little improved from the rain of the previous day, but fortunately it cleared by 10 a.m.. The three attacking companies busied themselves with preparations. Fighting order was worn, which meant that the infantry was not overburdened with heavy equipment. Gas masks, haversacks, water bottles and entrenching tools were discarded. Each platoon had a section of bomb throwers, each of which carried 10 Mills Bombs. A special section of rifle grenadiers were attached, each carrying six rifle grenades. One man in each section carried a smoke bomb. Six batteries of 6-inch howitzers and one of 60-pdrs. had been allocated to carry out a final bombardment of Narrow Trench as the attack went in. A curtain of shellfire would fall on three sides of the area to be attacked, which aimed to completely cut off this ground from any attempt by the Germans to reinforce. The fourth side of this box, facing the attackers, would be covered by a creeping barrage that moved ahead of the raiders. A final machine gun barrage from 72 guns, each firing 250 rounds of ammunition a minute, would fire over the heads of the attacking infantry and into the enemy positions. At 4 p.m., the final crescendo of artillery including high explosive and smoke shells, would crash down upon the unfortunate German defenders. After two minutes, the guns would lift from Narrow Trench and the creeping barrage would move forward at 100 yards per minute.

Exactly to the minute, the final barrage began from artillery, mortars and machine guns. 'A', 'B' and 'C' Companies clambered from their trenches and began the advance across no man's land. 'A' Company was on the left, 'C' Company was in the centre and 'B' Company was on the right. Roland's insistence upon the highest standards of training and preparation were about to show results.

The advance was made in platoon waves, each led by its commanding officer in the centre and the NCOs on the flanks. After the first wave had moved 15 yards, the second wave left the trench, followed by the third and fourth waves at intervals of ten yards. The infantry advanced in rushes from shell hole to shell hole, exposing themselves for the minimum amount of time. As they advanced, they fired their rifles and Lewis guns from the hip. The lines had not moved far when a German machine gun opened up, but the companies had prepared for this. The bombers in the advancing lines moved quickly towards the machine gun position, throwing bombs and crawling towards the target. The gunner was killed and the gun brought back to the British lines. Confused by the surprise attack and the measures used by the British to blind their artillery counter-barrage, the Germans were unable to retaliate for a few minutes. When their artillery did open fire, it proved to be ragged and much of it fell on the dummy infantry and tanks set up prior to the raid.

Overhead an R.E.8 of 12 Squadron (12 Wing) flown by Capt. D.F. Stevenson MC, with Lt. J. Webster as his observer, watched the infantry advance. They described the British artillery barrage as a wall of fire with no stray shells, which completely cut off the area of the attack. The infantry advancing behind the creeping barrage reached the enemy trench with only one casualty. The German infantry suffered heavy casualties. The barrage was so intense that most of the enemy officers and men were taking shelter in deep dugouts as the jubilant Durhams arrived in Narrow Trench. The Germans who refused to come out when ordered to do so died in their holes as explosives were thrown into the dugouts. An attempted enemy counter-attack was destroyed by British shellfire before they could get to close quarters. By 4.30 p.m., the raid was over and the companies returned to the British lines. By now the enemy artillery had recovered and was shelling no man's land through which the Durhams were retiring, but not with great success. The 9th Battalion had killed 70 Germans and taken 25 prisoners, while battalion losses were only 8 killed and 12 wounded. 'C' Company of the 8th Battalion re-entered Narrow Trench at 7.40 p.m. and caught the enemy attempting to clear up and reorganise the trench. A number of Germans were killed and three prisoners taken.

The family book has the following quotation from an unnamed eyewitness:

One figure…stood out prominently on the parapet at zero-hour, that of our beloved Colonel, who was helping the men out of the trench. He went forward into No Man's Land to see his boys reach their objective, and afterwards doubled back through the enemy barrage, to telephone his report to the General. He had asked permission to lead the men over, but had been forbidden to do so. But he would not be denied the pleasure of seeing the boys enter the enemy line.

Roland sent his usual end-of-action report to Brigade, part of which stated:

Objectives all gained. Some prisoners captured (76th I.R. [Infantry Regiment] and 167 I.R.), about 70 Germans killed. Two dugout entrances successfully blown in …Casualties slight.

Germans put down a heavy barrage on our Front Line and another on Bullfinch Support from Zero + 5 till Zero + 45. All enemy fire has now ceased. Raid was a complete surprise and our barrage perfect. Front line of left company was held up by MG and rifle fire from Narrow Trench about 0.26. c. 42.60 but bombers worked round on the left and the successful advance of our centre company, caused Germans to cease their resistance. No enemy coloured lights were observed – Germans made a feeble bombing attack on block in Narrow Trench at 0. 26. c. 25.12 which was bloodily repulsed. No Man's Land is good going and no obstacles were encountered.

Enemy wire presented no obstacle as gaps were frequent. At night however, the wire would prevent a slight obstacle and infantry would have to force their way through it unless they could discern the gaps.

This report was followed by Roland's analysis of action, which he was always at pains to forward to higher authority:

Formation: It was found in many cases that the Sections had to close up to get through the best gaps in the enemy wire. Instead of the assaulting troops being in four lines with the men extended to five paces, it would have been better for the first line only to be extended and for the remaining Sections (of the other three lines) to be closed up in file. In this way full use would still be made by the front line of their rifles in firing from the hip during the advance and the supporting lines would be under more efficient control and more able to negotiate easily any obstacles. If enemy rifle and machine gun fire was encountered, the Section columns could readily extend into line. If it were necessary for any Section to be diverted to an unexpected enemy post during the advance, this could easily be done if the troops were in the formation I have suggested.

In the withdrawal, most of the Sections came back in columns. Several had to extend owing to machine gun fire.

It is undoubtedly wise for troops to move back in Section columns. They are under better control and, in most barrages, there are gaps or thin parts through which a Section can dart and the section can always extend at once if fired on by machine guns or rifles. Men are always more confident when they are shoulder to shoulder with each other...

Hip Firing: All ranks attach great importance to firing from the hip during the advance...Firing on the move gives confidence to our men and takes their attention from the dangers which surround them. It gives the enemy the idea that they can be seen and are being aimed at, and makes them keep under cover.

Our Lewis Guns fired from the hip with the aid of slings. I consider that the Lewis Gun is too cumbersome for this method of firing and it would be better placed in the Second Line as has previously been the case.

Training: The practices over the Replica were of paramount importance. Every N.C.O. was provided with a good map. The splendid and up-to-date air photographs were of great help.

Surprise: The enemy were completely surprised. For operations of this nature it would be seen to be wise to have no previous heavy artillery preparation.

Wire: Enemy wire was well cut and good gaps were frequent. At night, unless unusually bright, the obstacle would have presented difficulty to assaulting troops.

Clearing our Front System: Heavy enemy barrages on our front and support lines and communication trenches might always be expected. If avoidable no one at all should remain in our front and support lines and the communications trenches should not be used. The plan of coming back across the open to Héninel proved an excellent one. The sooner our raids get clear of the front system the better.

Regimental Aid Post: The selection of the R.A.P. should be left to a Battalion Commander – subject, of course, to the approval of the Brigadier...The siting of the R.A.P. is a question of tactics...Most Doctors have stout hearts and are anxious to go where they think they will be of most use – regardless of danger. The safest position and the best dugout available near the line should be selected as an R.A.P., and the M.O. should rarely leave this place...

Trench Mortars: If avoidable Trench Mortars should not be in the trenches. These trenches are bound to come in for heavy fire in the ordinary course of any operation. The position, it is true, is governed mainly by their range, which unfortunately is small. The Trench Mortars should be sited clear of any trench and as far behind the front line as the range will allow. A deep shell hole can readily be converted into an emplacement and ammunition store. These places would be camouflaged until required and after the operation could be abandoned. Ammunition dumps should be separated from the Mortars by traverses and each dump should be divided into sections separated from each other by traverses. About three weeks notice was given of this operation and the Trench Mortar Personnel had plenty of time to work on their emplacements. If dummy positions had been carefully prepared during the past months, the enemy would probably have dispersed his artillery fire more.

Miscellaneous: The importance of having snipers to cover blocks was emphasised. Our snipers shot several Germans...

Covering parties: Covering parties on the flanks in No Man's Land were of great assistance to the Raiders. These parties kept up an effective fire throughout and covered the withdrawal very ably. Each party took 60 rifle bombs and it was found that double that number would have been able to be used effectively.

The amount of small arms ammunition and rifle bombs carried by the Raiders was just right. Some men fired 100 rounds of S.A.A. All rifle bombs were fired. The rifle bomb carrier used was very successful.

This report, as with all other reports written by Roland, shows his eye for detail, his courage to place his views before those of high-ranking officers, and his receptive mind that enabled him to learn from experience.

Following the raid, Roland wrote to thank Lt. Col. Martin, Commanding Officer of the 8th Battalion DLI:

The kindness you showed us and the assistance you gave us in getting in and out of our trenches, and all your efforts after the Raid in collecting our dear boys who were killed, are deeply appreciated by all Ranks of the Battalion which I command. Your Company in carrying out their Raid in the evening had an infinitely more difficult task than we, and all of us are full of admiration for the splendid way in which your men executed the Raid.

Roland also received a number of thanks and plaudits. Lt. Col. Karslake, G.S.O. 50th Division, observed the raid and wrote to Roland:

In case it should interest you, I should like to tell you what I saw of your gallant lads on Saturday.

Almost simultaneously with the first burst of artillery fire, they were swarming out of the front line.

They walked forward slowly. I could see some men shooting from the hip. Officers walked about slowly as they directed the men to the various gaps in the Boche wire. Once through that, they appeared on top of Narrow Trench. The men on the right were the first to arrive and they immediately began to fire from the shoulder, standing up, at what I imagine were Boche running away on the left.

Very soon most of them had disappeared but some, including an officer, spent the whole time walking up and down on top of Narrow Trench as if nothing imminent was happening.

Then about three Boche and two of our men came back towards Lone Sap and were followed at once by two Boche and one of our men from the direction of Brown Mound. From that direction also came what I thought to be a runner carrying a board. He jumped into our front line just short of Short Alley.

I only saw one man move out of a walk, and he came from the extreme left some minutes after the front lines had got back from the wire. He doubled along towards Byker Sap and suddenly dropped. I was afraid he was hit , but he picked himself up and got in safely, having evidently been tripped by the wire.

I was greatly relieved to see two stretcher bearers returning with the stretchers over their shoulders. Then I left, having seen one of the finest examples of discipline that anyone could wish to see.

Please accept my sincerest congratulations.

Brig. Gen. Cameron passed on the following remarks received from the GOC Third Army:

With reference to the raid carried out by the 50th Division on the 15th instant, the following remarks of the Third Army Commander are forwarded for the information of all concerned, 'An excellent raid full of originality and thought. The conduct of all who took part is most praiseworthy'.

The ultimate outcome of the raid may well have been 'the icing on the cake' for Roland in terms of promotion. The planning and leadership that had gone into the action, which was carried out by a highly disciplined and well-trained battalion, was not lost on Roland's superiors. Roland was not the only one to benefit – shortly after the raid Brig. Gen. Cameron of 151 Brigade was promoted to a divisional command for his participation in the action. The raid certainly clinched a command post for Roland, but the decision would not be announced for several weeks.

After a spell at rest, the 9th Battalion moved back into the front line. On the 25th September Roland took over temporary command of 151 Brigade in the absence of Brig. Gen. Cameron, who was probably on leave. On relinquishing temporary command, Roland went on leave to Paris. He wrote to his brother George:

I have just returned from four days' leave in Paris. It was a pleasant period. I can now speak French passing well! My good luck has continued. Although a C.O. now has no better chance of surviving than any of his men. The Americans I have seen have all been a keen, well set-up body, who appreciate all we have done, and who are anxious to learn all they can. The morale of our soldiers is very high, and their efficiency is of an excellent standard. Our ally Russia has indeed proved a broken reed. I suppose you have never thought of entering Parliament. There should be a great opportunity in politics after the War for an honest man to get on and do most interesting work. There would be a great public leaning towards service men, and if you decide on such a career you might one day become 'The Ruler of the King's Navee'.

I was interested to hear that you have pulled stroke in the two crews. My own condition is soft, and I fear I could not go even a couple of two-minute rounds with you.

I hope to get leave in December.

After returning from Paris, Roland went back to his battalion for what would be his last visit before taking up his new post. The 9th was in Saragossa Farm

Camp near Boesinghe providing working parties. On the 28th October, the battalion moved to Marsouin Camp for training. On the 4th November, it moved into the line in the Ypres Salient, with its headquarters at Egypt House. Here, it suffered from heavy enemy artillery fire. An unnamed officer observed of Roland:

Brigadier General Roland Bradford, 1917.

> During his last visit to his battalion in their shell hole posts, before receiving the news of his promotion to Brigadier General, he had reached the extreme left post and was talking to the Company Commander when a German machine gun opened out. About the third bullet pierced the Company Commander's steel helmet and the splinters from it wounded our Colonel in the face. He simply got up and said to the Company Commander, 'Are you hurt? What an idiot I was not to get down when I heard the first shot!'
>
> Being satisfied that his companion was alright, he walked back to get his wounds dressed.

Roland remained on duty, though it must have been an unpleasant and painful wound. He wrote to his Thomas the following day, but with characteristic modesty did not mention his wound:

> I have been appointed a Brig. Gen. (Temporary) to command the 186th Infantry Brigade, B.E.F., France.
>
> This came as a surprise.
>
> I hope you are keeping well. For the next week or two I will be very busy. So do not expect any letter. Perhaps you will be kind enough to forward this letter to Georgie when next you write.

Roland says little about how he felt about his promotion. He must have been proud, as the youngest man ever to become a Brigadier General at the remarkable age of 25, but he had mixed emotions about leaving the 9th. The family book details the changeover:

> Although notice of his appointment to command a Brigade was sent up to Lt. Col. Bradford and he was ordered to report at Divisional Headquarters, two or three days passed without him putting in an appearance. Eventually the Division phoned the Brigade and the D.A.A.G. said, 'Where the devil is Bradford? Here we have been trying to get him a Brigade for the last six months, and now he has got one he won't go to it!' Bradford insisted on remaining with his battalion until it was relieved and then he left us to take up his new command.

The interesting thing about this quote from Division is that Roland's superiors had been looking for a post for him for some time. Had one been available, it is possible that Roland would have been an even younger Brigadier General.

Roland's Second in Command, Maj. Crouch, was taking over command of the 9th Battalion. At the time that Roland was summoned, Maj. Crouch was on leave and it was quite obvious that Roland was reluctant to leave the battalion without a commander, particularly as his men were in the front line in the notorious and dangerous Ypres Salient. However, higher authority would not wait. Roland wrote to Maj. Crouch on the 6th November in a letter that shows the high regard he held for his Second in Command:

> My Dear Crouch,
>
> A message has just reached me stating that I have been appointed a Brig. Gen. to command 186 Inf. Bde. It is sad news for me, and is only alleviated by the knowledge that the Battalion will have in you such a splendid C.O. I will not attempt to tell you how greatly I shall miss you as a true friend and wise counsellor. Had it not been for your help I would never have been able to command the battalion successfully. But I will wait until I see you – which I hope will not be long – before expressing my gratitude and feelings generally. I am handing over to Rigg of 5th Borders who will command till I come back. You should finish your leave. I expect you will make Palmer your 2nd in Command. I have given Gee a list of N.C.Os whom I had intended to recommend for commissions. Unfortunately, Sgt. Crowe was slightly wounded today. I would like you to try and push him through for a commission at home if it can be worked.
>
> Two days ago I had written to the Brigade recommending Harker, Wylie and Innes for the position of 2nd in Command of a Battalion. Wylie, as you know is a splendid all-round officer and I hope you will see that he gets on well. If recommendations had been called for, I had decided to recommend the Doc [Capt.Scott] for a Brevet. As I told you some time ago, I had arranged to promote Sgt. Attey to C.S.M. in first vacancy.
>
> I was slightly wounded again yesterday – a mere scratch. So you will be seeing my name on the casualty list. The Doc is to be granted leave commencing on Nov. 11th. Inman slipped into hospital the other day whilst he was back at the Details Camp.
>
> The Battalion is not likely to be doing anything very important for the next week or two. It is a great rush for me to get away, and I will write you again when I get to the other end. I received your note about Cpl. Warden. It is a great pity that his brother is so ill. Lisle has been doing quite well during the few hard days we have had.
>
> I hope your cold is getting better, and that the family are all well.
>
> My kindest wishes, au revoir.
>
> Yours very sincerely,
>
> Roland Bradford

As promised, Roland wrote again to Maj. Crouch on the 9th November:

> Today I said Au Revoir to the Battalion. You can understand what my feelings were. It is like leaving home. Mind you make the most of your leave.
>
> The Division I am going to is a long way from the Battalion. But you may be sure that

I will come over and see you at the first opportunity, and after the War I hope to have the pleasure of meeting Mrs. Crouch and the family.

You will probably be seeing the Doc who will give you all the news. Everyone in the Battalion is delighted that you have got command and they will support you devotedly. Mind you get your Lt. Colonelcy fixed up right away, so that if you should be unfortunate enough to be laid off for a month or two, you will keep the rank.

Tyndale has just joined 6 D.L.I. as 2nd in Command. In the list of N.C.Os whom I consider fit for commission, which I left with Gee, I omitted the name of Cpl. Warden. But it is foolish of me to tell you these things, for you know the lads just as well as I do.

I am having a Souvenir Picture made and when they are ready, I will have 2,650 sent to you. Will you please cause one to be given to each N.C.O, Officer and Man who has ever served in the Battalion. There will be an envelope with each one. If 2,650 are not enough, please let me know and I will have more done.

Please give my best wishes to your family. I hope you are feeling better now.

May God keep you and help you.

The souvenir mentioned was an illustration of the regimental hymn 'Abide with Me', which Roland had commissioned specially for the men of the 9th Battalion. On the 8th November, Roland had written to Messrs. Raphael Tuck & Sons Ltd of Raphael House, Moorfields, City, London approving the finished picture and suggesting amendments:

In reply to the attached letter I think your artist has succeeded in making an excellent picture.

There is one alteration I wish. The soldier should be wearing a Box Respirator in the "alert" position – that is in front of his chest. The enclosed sketch shows this. Perhaps your artist could get some soldier on leave (at Victoria) to show him the exact position.

You will notice I have put a diamond on the right sleeve. In my Battalion we wear a small green diamond patch on the arms. If this could be added I would like it to be done – although it is not important.

I wish the words 'Abide with me' to be written over the top of the picture. In my Battalion we have a custom of singing this Hymn before going into action – and each day at dusk. The D.L.I. Crest should be put above the words 'Abide with me'. Only the Crest need to be shown and not the number of the Battalion.

The underneath – copied from my own handwriting which you will now find at the foot of the picture: With best wishes from Roland Bradford.

I think the D.L.I. Crest would be better done plain than embossed in gold, as gold would make it look rather gaudy.

I have been appointed a Brig. Gen. My address in future will be:

> Brig. Gen. R.B. Bradford,
> Cmdg. 186th Infantry Brigade,
> B.E.F. (France).

I do not wish the card to be a Christmas Card, but a souvenir picture from me to my Lads. So there will now be simply the D.L.I. Crest, 'Abide with me' and 'With best wishes from Roland Bradford' to be shown.

"ABIDE WITH ME"

With Best Wishes from Roland Bradford

Printed after his death, the signature on these cards could not have been Roland's. It is possible that the printers copied his signature and greeting from his letter, or that his mother provided a forgery.

As it will probably be framed by many – then I would like the picture to be fairly large, as large if possible as the specimen. But this I leave entirely to you.

Although I have suggested the position on the picture for the Crest, etc. to be printed, I wish your artist to use his own discretion absolutely, and if he thinks it would be better to change the positions, let him do so.

I want three thousand and agree to the price quoted, and will send you cheque as soon as possible.

When the picture (and envelopes) are completed, please send 2,650 to the:

Officer Commanding 9th Durham Light Infantry,

B.E.F. France.

The other 350, please send to me at new address. The cards to the 9th D.L.I. should be sent in packages of about 200 each.

Please complete and deliver as early as possible.

I feel confident that you will spare no effort to turn out a fine picture. It is for a good cause.

The cards would take more than six weeks to print and prepare.

Roland left his beloved battalion on the 9th November, with the following message:

> Comrades, we have endured many hardships together and it is against my wish that I leave you, but as a soldier I must obey orders. I asked permission to stay with you till the end of the war, and no honours or promotion can ease the ache in my heart on leaving you. When the war is over, I hope we may meet again to talk over the days when we fought together.

Brig. Gen. Roland Boys Bradford took command of 186 Brigade, 62nd (West Riding) Division on the 10th November 1917. He had replaced Brig. F.F. Hill CB, CMG, DSO who had retired due to age restrictions. Roland introduced himself to his brigade with the following speech:

> Comrades, I come to introduce myself to you as your new Brigadier. This is the first

opportunity I have had to speak to you today. I am going to ask you to put your implicit trust and confidence in me; to look upon me not only as your Brigadier, but as your friend. By the help of God I will try to lead you to the best of my ability, and remember your interests are my interests. As you all know, a few days from now we are going to attack. Your powers are going to be tested. They must not fail you. Above all, pray! More things are wrought by prayer than this world dreams of! It is God alone who can give us victory and bring us through this battle safely.

The battle that faced Roland in his new command was the Battle of Cambrai, the plans for which were already well advanced. It was to be the first major tank battle in history with the nearly 500 tanks British of all types leading five divisions east of the Canal du Nord. The area of the battle lay in the undulating grassland, dotted by woods and fortified villages, six miles deep and seven miles wide between the Canal du Nord on the west and the Canal d'Escaut on the east.

The 62nd Division had already commenced its training for the battle in early November near Wailly, four miles southeast of Arras. This involved demonstrations of how tanks could cut through wire defences and assault enemy trenches. Coordination between tanks and infantry on this scale was an entirely new idea, and needed particular attention. The role of aircraft as part of a major battle was also examined and practiced. Roland arrived on the 10th of the month when most of the training had already taken place, and had a lot of catching up to do in a very short period of time. It is a measure of his genius that he immediately saw how he would work with the tanks and would have noted already that, at last, the ultimate means of leading infantry across no man's land in some safety had arrived. He went personally to meet with the tank commanders to discuss the best methods of mutual support between armour and infantry. Roland had long held the opinion that tanks should move forward with the infantry in close support. Months previous in a letter dated 29th April 1917, he made his thoughts on tanks known to his Brigade Commander:

> They [the tanks] should go with the infantry. This gives confidence to our men and helps to demoralise the enemy. If they came on later the enemy is more prepared and will be able to devote more attention of his artillery to dealing with them.
>
> I consider that tanks might be used extensively for carrying of artillery ammunition and also stores for infantry – Stokes Gun Ammo. Etc. Cannot smoke barrages be established to hamper observation?

Roland was fortunate that the 62nd Division was commanded by Maj. Gen. Walter Braithwaite who welcomed the tanks and was anxious to find out what they could do, unlike Maj. Gen. Harper GOC 51st Division on his immediate right, who was suspicious of this new weapon and failed to give his tanks close infantry support. Maj. Gen. Harper's scepticism led to great difficulties on the first day of action, and his division failed to take the village of Flesquières, a first-day objective, and thus created an open right flank for the 62nd Division. Maj. Gen. Braithwaite, however, saw the potential of the tanks to cross no man's land and clear a way through the dense wire in front of the Hindenburg Line, enabling him to take on enemy machine gun fire and destroy it.

The objectives of the 62nd Division at Cambrai were those sections of the Hindenburg Line that lay ahead of the attacking brigades, Havrincourt Village, Craincourt and Anneux. Maj. Gen. Braithwaite was to attack with two of his three brigades. These were the 185 on the right and the 187 on the left. Roland's brigade was in reserve with orders to pass through the two other brigades when they had reached their objectives, and continue the advance to gain the line from Graincourt to the factory on the Bapaume–Cambrai road. Roland's brigade was also to take the Hindenburg Support system and occupy Anneux, and link up with the 1st Cavalry Division on the right by taking the high ground west of Bourlon Wood. In support were the 1st King Edward's Horse (less one squadron) and a company of tanks from 'G' Battalion. On learning of his role, Roland asked permission of his divisional commander to place his brigade as far forward as possible in order to launch his advance quickly after the frontal brigades has reached their objectives. Too often the mistake had been made of holding reserves too far back and by the time they arrived at the front the enemy had recovered and stopped the advance. Roland believed in speed of action, keeping the impetus of the attack moving whilst the enemy was reeling from the first assault. Maj. Gen. Braithwaite wrote:

> The night before the battle, Bradford was very anxious to advance early on the 20th and take up a much more forward position. It was the ardour of youth and there was a great deal in it if things went right. But, of course, the whole plan of the battle was at the time rather a striking departure from anything that had been done before…I did not, therefore, fully concur with Bradford, nor did I like being without some sort of reserve. I felt, however, that there was a great deal in what Bradford said, and therefore I decided that at any rate I would go some of the way with his idea, in fact, I decided to 'chance my arm', and so I gave him instructions to keep moving forward, and directly the leading brigades had gained their initial success (which we hoped for and anticipated with a certain amount of confidence) that the 186th Brigade should push through. It was taking a bit of a risk, but if it came off it was well worth it. As a matter of fact, it did come off and had a tremendous effect on the fortunes of the day alone, because Bradford was a born leader and led his Brigade with conspicuous success.

Total surprise was achieved on the morning of the 20th November. At zero hour (6.30 a.m.) and with no preliminary bombardment, the tanks crawled forward followed by the infantry and the powerful Hindenburg Line was pierced and broken. The 185 and 187 Brigades of the 62nd Division moved towards their objectives. The 185 Brigade had taken its first objectives of the Hindenburg front trenches, and had taken the village of Havrincourt by 10.15 a.m. The 187 Brigade reached its second objective before 10.30 a.m. and had cleared the Hindenburg Line to where it crossed over to the west bank of the Canal du Nord. It was now the time for 186 Brigade to continue the advance. Perfectly placed to do this the four battalions of the Duke of Wellingtons Regiment (2/4th, 2/5th, 2/6th, and

2/7th) leapfrogged through and moved quickly towards the brigade's objectives. Roland, not one for sitting in his headquarters waiting for information, was on the move all day. Whenever there was a hold up, he appeared in order to solve the problem and inspire his troops to greater effort. The Official History gives an example of his energy and his style of command:

> Brig. Gen. Bradford having come forward to keep control of the advance, ordered an attack on Graincourt by the two companies of 2/4th Duke of Wellingtons already in position, such tanks as were present to lead the way.

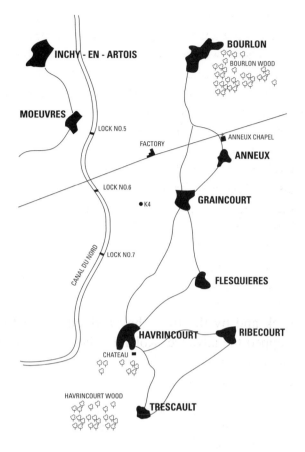

The Cambrai battle, November 1917.

Graincourt fell but a problem that had arisen on the right flank threatened to hold up the advance. The failure of the 51st Division to take Flesquières had left the 62nd Division open to enemy enfilade fire. Maj. Gen. Braithwaite ordered the advance to stop and that all available tanks be moved back and sent to Flesquières, so attacking this village from the west. Again, the Official History quotes:

> If, as seems doubtful, Br-General Bradford received this order, he saw no reason why it should deflect him from the attack on his immediate objective. He lost no time in pushing troops forward towards Anneux and to the factory buildings on the Cambrai road

Anneux was reached and the factory buildings taken but, as darkness was falling, it was considered advisable to withdraw to the area of Graincourt for the night. Roland visited the 27th Battalion and spurred them on to continue their attack down the Hindenburg trenches, using bomb and bayonet to clear them of the enemy. There were numerous deep dugouts and it took until 10 p.m. to complete the task. German resistance had increased as the day wore on and they overcame their initial surprise. The 2/5th Battalion stormed an enemy strongpoint in the grounds of Havrincourt Chateau and had lost its commanding officer. It continued the advance behind tanks to its final objective, a trench beyond the

Bapaume–Cambrai road. The advance of the brigade is estimated as over four miles, arguably the longest advance by a brigade since the early days of the war.

Roland's headquarters were now established in the catacombs of Graincourt church. Three German army engineers were captured and were put to work ensuring that the electric lights equipment continued to operate. Here he received a visit from a number of very cold and soaked tank officers who would be working with him on the following day. Not all of the infantry commanders received tank commanders with such understanding and with a desire to work with them, but within just days of being in command Roland had grasped the idea and was able to issue very clear orders for their use. There were many, such as Maj. Gen. Harper, who harboured suspicion of tanks and misunderstanding of what they could do. Roland was not one of these. He had grasped how effective tanks could be against enemy trench defences and the positive effect they had on his troops' morale. Roland insisted that his visitors eat, drink and warm themselves before discussing how to move against the objectives set for the following day, the 21st November. These were the capture of Bourlon Village and Wood. A.J. Smithers in his book *Cambrai: The First Great Tank Battle 1917* wrote:

> In a letter Colonel Oldfield remarked that his Brigadiers in the 51st [Division] were the best in the Army. Admirable though they were, there was a Brigadier of Braithwaite's who stood head and shoulders above the rest. Boys Bradford, 25 years old, commander of an infantry brigade and holder of the Victoria Cross, was not of the common run of men., his brigade was ordered up from Graincourt to the assault on Bourlon; his battalions could not have been better chosen. Bradford was the ideal General for work of this kind.

In the spirit of co-operation with his tank commanders, Roland worked through orders for the use of the tanks. On the following day, led by the tanks of 'G' Battalion (I Tank Brigade), the battalions of 186 Brigade moved forward. The 2/4th Duke of Wellington's entered Anneux and took Anneux Chapel after heavy fighting. The Lewis gunners of the battalion advanced firing from the hip, which effectively dealt with enemy troops firing from the houses. The 2/7th Battalion advanced about 1,000 yards before being held up by thick wire. The 2/5th had the difficult task of bombing along the Hindenburg Support system. By nightfall it had reached a point in this trench system about 700 yards east of the Canal du Nord. An enemy counter-attack at 8 p.m. was beaten off. The 2/6th Battalion was ordered to pass through the 2/7th and attack Bourlon village. Roland issued the orders to this battalion that 'The Village must be thoroughly mopped up'. Having learned from past mistakes, Roland ensured that when enemy trenches and strong points had been taken the dugouts and hidden shelters of enemy troops would not be able to use their rifles and machine guns to fire into the backs of the advancing troops.

Enemy opposition was now intensely strong and Bourlon Wood and Village could not be taken. The Official History stated:

> Br-General Bradford's 186th Brigade had accomplished as much as could be fairly expected. Against an increasing resistance, with very little support, it had striven for an objective which might have taxed the power of a fresh division.

At the end of the first two days of fighting, Roland's brigade had captured 8 officers, 1,130 other ranks, 34 field guns, 38 machine guns and a trench mortar.

The 62nd Division was relieved and went into rest. In the following days the British were able to capture part of Bourlon Wood. On the 26th November, the 62nd Division was called up to take over the assault on the remaining areas of the Wood and to take the village. The 186 Brigade moved forward through Hermes and crossed the Canal du Nord by Lock No. 7 and moved into position. The 185 Brigade was on Roland's right and 187 on the left. The attack commenced at 6.20 a.m. on the 27th November. The brigade held a position just below the crest of the ridge that ran through the centre of the Wood. Immediately in front of it, the Wood comprised dense undergrowth and visibility was down to about 20 yards. German resistance was intense, and the skilled and resolute enemy bitterly contested every yard of ground. By 4.30 p.m., the brigade occupied positions along the Bourlon Village road. The enemy counter-attacked several times, and though these were broken up it soon became clear that the positions held were becoming untenable. The brigade chose to retire to the high ground in the rear.

On the night of the 28th/29th November, the 62nd Division was relieved by the 47th (London) Division. Roland and his brigade marched back to positions east of the Canal du Nord, just south of Lock No. 6 [map reference K4d]. Between 9 and 10 a.m., as was his usual practice, Roland left his headquarters to visit his troops. At first his headquarters staff had no real concern for his whereabouts – when out of line Roland spent a few hours every day talking to the men. But when he had not returned by early afternoon, a search party was sent out to find him. At about 2 p.m. he was found lying dead. He had been killed by a piece of shrapnel from a stray shell, which had pierced his spine.

Maj. Gen. Braithwaite issued the following order a day or two after Roland's death.

> It is with the deepest regret that the Divisional Commander has to announce that Brigadier General R.B. Bradford VC, MC, (DLI), commanding the 186th Infantry Brigade, was killed in action on November 30th.
>
> Though General Bradford has been so short a time in command of the 186th Brigade, the exploits of that Brigade in their wonderful advance on the 20th November and succeeding days will ever be associated with his name, no less than will the fighting and consolidation in Bourlon Wood.
>
> The 62nd (West Riding) Division is the poorer by the loss of so gallant and determined a leader and the Army can ill afford to lose a soldier of real genius such as was our late comrade.

Roland was later buried in Hermes Military Cemetery. Maj. Gen. Walter Braithwaite wrote:

He was a very exceptional man, though only a boy, and might have risen, in fact would have risen, to any height in his profession. His power of command was quite extraordinary. He certainly knew every officer in his Brigade, although he had only commanded it for quite a short time, and I honestly believe he knew every non-commissioned officer, and a great many of the privates. He had extraordinary personality, and that personality, linked with his undoubted military genius, made him a very extraordinary character and a very valuable commander of men. His services during the battle can hardly be too highly appraised.

The Maj. Gen. also wrote to the Commanding Officer of 151 Brigade on the 11th January 1918:

Bradford was only with me, as I daresay you know, for about a month, but during that time I and everybody else in the Division conceived a great admiration and affection for him and we all felt his loss very keenly. He did simply splendidly. I know very few men who, joining a Brigade so very short a time before battle as he did, could have got the splendid results that he did. He was quite indefatigable, he infused the whole of his Brigade with his own fine spirit of determination and of dash tempered with sound judgement. It was his Brigade that made that fine advance on Graincourt–Anneux and the Cambrai road and, later on in the fighting completed the capture of Bourlon Wood. His death was very sad for he had just gone out of his dugout to have a look round when he was caught and killed instantaneously by a stray shell – after the whole show was over – on November 30th. We buried him in Hermes. He was a very fine gallant Gentleman and I don't wonder that you who knew him so long, felt so much admiration for him. Personally I think he is the most remarkable character that I have met during this war. He had an absolute genius for war and a fine tactical instinct, and I think men would have gone anywhere for him. His loss is not only to his Division but to the whole army, for he would certainly have gone far.

Another officer of Roland's brigade paid tribute, writing:

He had only been with us a short time, but he had already endeared himself by his exceptional charm of manner to every officer and man in the Brigade. He inspired the most wonderful confidence in everyone, and the men would have gone anywhere for him. We have lost a real friend and a great leader.

On the evening of the 30th November, the 9th Battalion Durham Light Infantry was in a training area west of Arras. It was ordered to fall in on parade, and the band was present. A visibly upset Lt. Col. Crouch told the assembled troops that Roland had been killed that day. After saying the Lord's Prayer, the band struck up 'Abide with Me', Roland's hymn that he had left as a legacy of his faith and command.

A measure of the continued loyalty and affection for Roland held by those members of the 9th Battalion who had served with him can be shown in a letter from Lance Corporal King, who had been Roland's servant from 1912:

The General let me go on three days' leave before they had to go into action on November 20th and I got back on December 2nd. The poor General was killed on November 30th, and the first words I spoke when I got back were to some of the men of his Brigade asking if he was all right. And they gave me the sad answer, and I can

Roland's original grave, c. 1918, and the modern headstone in Hermes Cemetary.

tell you it nearly broke my heart after being with him so long. I have been back nearly a fort-night and I can't get settled down at all; I feel as though I don't know where I want to be.

An anonymous member of the 9th Battalion recorded:

In December 1917, just a few weeks after they had learned of Bradford's death, the 9th Durhams left the horrors of the Ypres Salient and moved into billets. That night, after 'Last Post' was sounded, came 'Abide With Me'. A soldier, newly arrived in the Battalion sneered, 'What's this? A bloody Sunday school!' He was immediately punched to the ground by a veteran soldier wearing the ribbon of the Military Medal, Private Bobby Davidson, who told him, 'That hymn was taught to us by a better bloody soldier than you will ever be'.

The news of Roland's death reached the family. George wrote to his mother on the 5th December:

My dear Mother,

I received your telegram and am truly sorry for you. Roland had died a hero's death and we should all be honoured and proud that he was able to do so much for his country. You have the greatest honour of all to have produced such a son and to have given him the home training that has made him capable of so much.

We may be certain that he is not sorry and we must try and bear it with the same kind of fortitude he always displayed. He leaves a mark on British history that will go on for ever.

Best Love,

God comfort you,

Your affectionate son,

G.N. Bradford

On 21st December 1917, Roland's mother received a letter from Raphael Tuck & Sons Ltd:

> Will you allow us to extend our sincerest sympathy to you on your sad bereavement caused by the loss of your son, Brig. Gen. Bradford V.C.
>
> The nation has reason to mourn his loss as deeply because the mere fact that he attained his high position at the age of 25 is significant of the value place upon his services by a grateful King.
>
> No one is better able to judge of his kindness of heart than his Mother, but a letter written us by your son, under date 8th November, of which we beg to enclose a typed copy, giving evidence as it does of his thoughtfulness to all his men under him will, we have no doubt, be appreciated by you.
>
> With it we enclose a copy of the picture referred to in the letter and which we have the gratification of preparing for him, but which we have not produced any further.
>
> With the expression of our hope that the season and New Year to follow will bring you balm and peace.

Though he did not live to see the finished picture he commissioned, Roland's mother ensured that a copy was sent to every man who had served in the 9th Battalion with Roland. The framed picture hung from the walls in many homes in the years following the end of the war.

George wrote to sister Amy on the 22nd December 1917:

> Poor old Roland will live in history, a marvellous leader of men and died a glorious death…There was a small paragraph in *The Times* saying that it was intended to open a fund to commemorate the career of Brigadier General Bradford VC. Mr Pike Pease being appointed Treasurer.
>
> I had also told Harrod's to send some chocs to Roland just before I knew about his death…

Along with the family messages, tributes were written for Roland from all sectors of the army. No less a person than Sir Douglas Haig, commander of the British Army in France, wrote in 1918:

> I knew Bradford quite well and personally followed his career with interest. He was an officer of outstanding talent and personality…exceptionally young but particularly capable. His death was a great loss to the Army and I and all who had known and served with him deeply deplore it…The example of his unselfish courage and devotion to duty is in my opinion, very worthy of being kept in continual remembrance by a nation he died to serve.

The author and historian John Buchan wrote an appreciation of Roland:

> It is customary, when we count the cost of war, to dwell especially upon the sacrifice of youth. The young men who would have shaped the future have perished in laying its foundations. Gifts of inestimable value to the world have been lost to it before they could find scope or fruition. Poets and thinkers have died, mute but not inglorious, men of action, statesmen, builders of society have passed before they could reveal them-

selves, leaving only an inheritance of 'unfulfilled renown.'

But there is another side to the tragedy. There are many of the dead whom we can think of as having been born for the Great War, as having always been in training for it. Boys fresh from school or college have found in a few years of campaigning a far richer career than most men who reach the full span of life.

It is possibly true to say that Roland Boys Bradford was one of these young men who was 'born for the Great War'.

Chapter 9

1918

The death of two of his brothers in 1917 did not stop George Bradford from stepping forward when volunteers were needed in early 1918 for what the Navy called a particularly dangerous mission.

The mission in question was a naval raid on the port of Zeebrugge, Belgium. Lying only 65 miles from the English coast and an uncomfortable 70 miles from Dover, Zeebrugge was capable of taking large ships as well as torpedo craft, destroyers and submarines, and the Germans were using these to inflict enormous losses on the main British shipping lanes and supply lines across the Channel and the Atlantic. The British navy periodically bombarded Zeebrugge, but to limited effect as the enemy kept shipping anchored in the harbour down to a minimum, commensurate with the needs of defence, mine laying and lightening raids on British shipping lanes. Zeebrugge was mainly used for access to the North Sea and English Channel from a safe haven at the inland port of Bruges. At the beginning of 1918, it was estimated that on any given day 18 submarines and 25 destroyers or torpedo boats lay at Bruges. The Zeebrugge–Bruges Canal, over six miles in length, was capable of taking warships up to light cruiser in size. In addition, Zeebrugge contained one of the Germans' largest seaplane bases in Flanders.

In 1917, the Admiralty came to the opinion that unless the Allies could recapture the French and Belgian coast from Ostend to Zeebrugge, the war against Germany could be lost. One of the objectives of Haig's Flanders campaign, which opened on 31st July 1917, was to drive the Germans from the coast and capture the ports. It was intended that, following the breakthrough of the German lines in the Ypres Salient, the army would thrust towards the Belgium coast. The army would meet up with a seaborne landing, and the coast – particularly the ports of Zeebrugge and Ostend – would be freed from enemy control. By the end of Third Battle of Ypres, more than 300,000 British casualties had bought only a handful of miles of Belgian territory in three and one-half months of bitter fighting in appalling conditions. The Belgium coast remained firmly in German hands.

The Admiralty had been looking at a number of ways to eradicate the German threat on the coast. These had included plans to bombard the harbour defences at Zeebrugge and its lock gates using heavy naval guns, to land military forces by sea onto the beaches close by and attempt to capture the lock gates and canal entrance, and to ram the lock gates using a blockship. Yet another plan suggested that forces could be landed on the harbour mole and attack along it into the town of Zeebrugge, destroying the lock gates and canal entrance from the town. In considering all of these, it was decided that the harbour and coastal defences were

Lt. Commander George Bradford aboard the Orion, c. 1917.

far too strong to guarantee any certainty of success. To understand this decision we need to examine the enemy defences.

A man-made harbour, Zeebrugge was formed by a mole of considerable size and strength to withstand the storms, tides and currents of the North Sea. The mole was built out from the coast about one-half mile west of the canal entrance and curves in a semi-circle north and eastward for over one and one-half miles. Its structure can be divided into four sections. The first is a causeway, built out from the coast for 250 metres and carrying a footway, roadway and a double rail track. The next section comprised a steel viaduct, about 300 metres in length, which continued the railway and footway. The viaduct had another vital role in that it enabled the currents to flow through it, preventing sand from silting up the harbour area. The third section was the major section of the mole. It was about 75 metres wide and 1,700 metres long. It was the site of the peacetime railway station and had dock installations for passengers and goods. The final section of the mole was 240 metres long and just under five metres wide. At the end of this section stood the lighthouse.

In addition to the length and strength of the wall, it was carefully guarded by artillery. Six guns of between 3.5-inch and 5.9-inch calibre were mounted on the final section of the mole nearest the lighthouse. These guns could fire out to sea and, it was believed, could also be swivelled to fire into the harbour and coast if necessary. On the third and broadest section of the mole was a battery of 5.9-inch guns sited to fire at any vessels that rounded the lighthouse and attempted to enter the harbour. On this section the Germans had also built concrete trenches and positions for anti-aircraft weapons and machine guns, together with blockhouses to accommodate about 1,000 men. All of these positions were surrounded by barbed wire. The railway station and warehouses had been converted into a seaplane base and depots for the supply and maintenance of ships and seaplanes. German warships on their way out to sea and returning to Bruges could be moored on the harbour side of the mole. Finally, the coastlines on both sides of Zeebrugge were defended by batteries of heavy guns and powerful trench systems, strongly wired in. There were also extensive minefields and shoals, which had remained unplotted and unmarked since the early days of the war.

Aerial photographs revealed a certain amount of silting of the harbour, which the enemy had not dredged. Immediately inside the harbour and running from the mole, were two protective booms with a gap between them. One of the booms comprised barges held by chains and, the other was of nets weighted to give them depth. The mouth of the canal leading to the lock gates was affected by silting, leaving a narrow central channel for the use of shipping. The banks of the canal up to the lock gates were defended by guns capable of firing at short range upon any ship attempting to enter the canal. The mouth of the canal was continued out to sea by two extended arms of wooden piers about 200 metres long. These curved to a point where the seaward ends measured over 180 metres apart. Any vessel attempting to enter the harbour and block the port had to round the lighthouse on the end of the mole, avoid the booms, navigate the narrow channel into the canal, manoeuvre into a blocking position across the canal, and be sunk in position. To top it off, the whole of the journey would have to be made under the noses of an alert enemy. It was obvious that a raid on Zeebrugge had to have planning and navigational skills of the very highest order.

The final plan presented to the Admiralty by Vice Admiral Keyes and agreed by their Lordships in mid-December 1917 included elements of previous plans. The powerful structure and defences of the mole and canal entrance at Zeebrugge were such that anything other than a surprise attack would fail with dire consequences. Essentially the plan was to sail three blockships into the mouth of the canal and sink these vessels in such a manner as to completely block the canal. To enable the blockships to sail unobserved past the lighthouse and the guns on the mole, it was planned that an attacking force of Royal Marine Light Infantry and Royal Bluejackets would create a diversion. These units would land on the mole and attack its garrison and gun positions, gaining the full attention of the defenders while the blockships slipped into the harbour.

To prevent the mole garrison from being reinforced from the shore, two submarines laden with high explosives were to ram the pillars of the viaduct, creating a gap too wide for German reinforcements to cross. Shore installations and guns were to be bombarded from the sea by monitors firing 15-inch guns, prior to and throughout the raid. Meanwhile, Zeebrugge itself was to be bombed from the air. Torpedo boats and destroyers would protect the considerable armada of ships from German retaliation from the sea. Motor launches and fast coastal motorboats were to rescue the crews of the blockships and the submarines. These boats were also to be used to lay down a dense smokescreen that, added to the darkness of the night, would blind the enemy on the mole to the approaching ships. Tide and weather were vital to the success of the raid. It was essential that a steady breeze was blowing towards the shore to carry the smoke with it. The fleet of ships would need to arrive in darkness, ideally with no moon and with high water between darkness and dawn. The assault was planned for April 1918, during which four or five nights in the middle of the month met the required conditions. It was finally decided that the appropriate dates would be between the 9th and 13th of April. The plan and date now agreed, a simultaneous attack was planned for Ostend.

The plan and date agreed, suitable ships now had to be found. For the Zeebrugge raid Vice Admiral Keyes required an assault vessel to lead the diversionary attack on the mole and three blockships to sail into the mouth of the canal. The light cruiser HMS Vindictive was available and earmarked for the assault role. The light cruisers HMS Thetis, Intrepid and Ipheginia were made available and prepared as blockships to seal the canal. All four ships were adapted to meet their particular roles. The Vindictive, commanded by Capt. A.B.F. Carpenter, carried the majority of the assault units. These were drawn from the Royal Marine Light Infantry and Royal Bluejackets. Fearful that the Vindictive might hit a mine on the journey over to Zeebrugge that would have ruined any possibility of success, it was decided to look for vessels of sufficient low draught to enable them to sail over minefields. These vessels would carry sufficient forces to allow the assault to go in with some prospect of success should disaster hit the Vindictive. The support vessels chosen were two Merseyside ferryboats, the Iris and the Daffodil which, in turn, were suitably converted for the difficult and dangerous task ahead. George Bradford was given command of the Royal Bluejackets assault unit, which would be carried on the Iris.

There was never any doubt in Vice Admiral Keyes' mind of the enormous dangers that would face all those who took part in the raid. He insisted that the crews of the blockships in particular should be single men, as their chances of surviving were very small indeed. All Keyes could offer them was at best was to spend the rest of the war in a German P.O.W. Camp – a more likely prospect was wounding or death. Plans had been made to rescue the crews using launches, which would follow the blockships into the mouth of the canal, but this was somewhat optimistic to say the least. The crews of the rescue vessels themselves would be in close range of enemy fire every step of the way and their own prospects of survival were slim. In early 1918, the Admiralty asked for volunteers from the various naval establishments and the fleet, without revealing the true nature of the enterprise or the objective but emphasising the extreme danger involved. There were more volunteers than places.

George Bradford was one of them. It would have been uncharacteristic if he head not taken up the challenge, and we can suppose his senior officers expected him to volunteer. After all, George had an alert mind and a strong and healthy body. The Chelmer incident had shown that he had courage and the mental capacity to make a quick decision and act upon it immediately, and he had spent most of the war in inactivity waiting for the opportunity for action. Jutland had only been a brief interlude and he suffered, along with others serving in the Grand Fleet, from the grumbles and jibes which came from the general public who anxiously awaited the invincible Royal Navy to show its teeth in this war. George had a further reason for wanting to get into action: two of his brothers had been killed in action on the Western Front. Here was an opportunity, at last, to exact some retribution on the enemy for his loss.

The main assault force to attack the mole was provided by the 4th Battalion Royal Marine Light Infantry, who would attack from the Vindictive. Two hundred Royal Blue Jackets were added to this force. Some of these had seen action with the Royal Naval Brigade and with the Royal Siege Guns in front of Dunkirk. Both of these units received additional training in attacking fixed positions similar to the trench systems in France, adding certainty to the common belief amongst the men that they were bound for the Western Front to attack a particular strongpoint. George Bradford and his detachment of Royal Blue Jackets underwent this training.

During the first days of April, men were moved from their training areas and accommodated in the Vindictive and the retired battleship Hindustan. Both were lying in the concentration area of the Swin, north of the Thames Estuary. They were then let in on the secret of their ultimate destination. On the 11th April 1918, in an atmosphere of intense excitement and tension and in suitable weather, the armada sailed from the Swin, led by the Vindictive. It was late afternoon and their immediate objective was to meet with the escorting vessels coming up from Dover at a point about seven miles east of Ramsgate. The whole armada was then to set sail for Zeebrugge. About 20 miles from Zeebrugge and with the final preparations for action taking place onboard, the weather changed. The vital on-shore breeze changed direction and began to blow towards the sea. There was now no chance of the smokescreen covering the approaching ships and hiding them from the enemy guns on the

An artist's impression of storming the mole at Zeebrugge, April 1918.

110

mole and the coast. Vice Admiral Keyes had no alternative but to order the armada back to the home base.

Two days later on the 13th April, the weather conditions were again considered suitable and the task force sailed out only to be disappointed once more. The wind quickly rose to gale force and the ships were again ordered back to base. It is not difficult to imagine the great disappointment and frustration amongst the keyed-up officers and men, and senior officers worried about the effect the setbacks were having upon morale. There was an even more pressing worry. Had surprise been lost? It was almost inconceivable that some passing merchant ship had failed to see the task force at sea, comprising as it did of hundreds of vessels of all sizes. It was obvious that something big was afoot and, intentionally or not, reports could have been picked up by German intelligence. If this had happened the Germans would have almost certainly considered that such a large force was heading for an amphibious landing somewhere on the Belgium coast. So warned, the enemy would be ready and waiting. In these circumstances would the Admiralty allow a third attempt? An essential consideration was that the raid would have to be made outside the period of darkness suitable for the crossing. Keyes considered it worth the risk and his persuasive powers won the day.

The next essential high tide arrived on the 22nd April. The weather in the early morning was not too encouraging but, with an inner feeling that all would be well, Keyes gave the order to sail. The breeze required to blow the intended smokescreen into the eyes of the waiting German garrison on the mole rose and stayed steady. The task force crossed the intervening sea without major incident and closed undetected on Zeebrugge. The smoke cloud was released and rolled in with the breeze to cover the mole. All seemed to be going according to plan. Yet when the Vindictive was about one-quarter mile from the mole, the breeze changed direction and the smoke clouds rolled back out to sea. The Vindictive followed by the Iris and the Daffodil had to race the short distance to the mole in full view of a now alert enemy, who responded to the sight of the British fleet by opening fire. Hit a number of times by enemy guns, the vessels steamed on until at one minute past midnight on the 23rd April – St. George's Day – the Vindictive reached the mole wall. Capt. Carpenter on the Vindictive wrote:

> She was sadly out of position. She rolled from side to side like a dinghy in a liner's wash and thus completed the ruin of the essential landing brows. Her speed through the shallow water had built up an enormous surge, now trapped between her side and the concrete mole, and thrashing to burst free. Up and down the waters leaped, forced up by the follow under-current, dropped back into the void left as the surge bounced away from the base of the mole; boiling up and spewing out again as the Vindictive bucked and reared in the turmoil.

It was impossible to land the assault parties under such conditions but the Daffodil saved the situation. Coming up alongside the Vindictive, the Daffodil pushed her nose into the Vindictive's side and nudged her up against the mole wall and held her there. The survivors of the assault parties, for many had been killed or wounded under the blistering fire from the enemy guns as the ship raced to the mole, rushed onto the mole and began the diversionary attack and tried to capture or destroy the enemy guns.

Meanwhile, the Iris with George Bradford and his assault party onboard steamed past the Vindictive and Daffodil and endeavoured to place herself alongside the mole. Protected by the high wall of the mole towering above her, she was not subjected at this stage to the violent enemy reaction from which the Vindictive was suffering. On the other hand, troops attacking from the Iris would make a perfect target for the enemy as they appeared above the parapet of the mole wall. The Iris rocked and pitched violently in the turbulent seas, making it impossible for the assaulting troops to lean scaling ladders against the wall, and many were smashed in an attempt to place them in position. Lt. Claude E.V. Hawkins, who had volunteered from HMS Erin, climbed a ladder held vertically by a number of men. He balanced himself on the top rungs, then leapt onto the parapet and attempted to secure the ladder. He was last seen using his revolver against the defenders, before he was shot and killed. The position was desperate. Unless the vessel could be secured to the mole wall to enable the remaining ladders to be placed in position, no one was going to get off the Iris to support the Vindictive's assault units already engaged on the mole.

George Bradford, fully realising the situation, climbed one of the derricks, which was heaving and swaying violently. It was an exceedingly dangerous and difficult climb, only made possible by his considerable strength and athleticism. He carried with him a parapet anchor. Judging the right moment to perfection as the derrick swayed towards the top of the wall, he leapt onto the parapet and tried to secure the anchor. In attempting doing this he was fatally shot by enemy fire and fell into the sea between the Iris and the mole. Petty Officer Hallihan saw him fall and dove into the sea in an attempt to save him, but to no avail. Hallihan lost his life also, but was later awarded a posthumous Mention In Despatches. George Bradford's body washed up on the beach near Blankenburg a few days later and was buried with full military honours by the Germans in Blankenburg Communal Cemetery, where it rests to this day. George Bradford was killed on his 31st birthday.

Two of the three blockships reached the mouth of the canal. Their bottoms were blown out and they were successfully sunk in position to block the entrance. The assault forces on the mole were taken off and the Vindictive and the two ferryboats limped back to England. Losses had been heavy but the raid had resulted in the restoration of the public's pride in the Royal Navy. It struck a chord with the British people who saw in it the spirit of the Elizabethan Sea Hawks and of Nelson. However, in reality, the success achieved was not as much as the Admiralty had hoped. The Germans dug a new route around the obstructions and the canal was soon operational again. The raid had little, if any, influence on the outcome of the war except that it lifted the morale of the officers and men, and the restored the British confidence in their Navy.

Initially five Victoria Crosses were awarded to officers and men who took part in the raid. George Bradford received a posthumous Mentioned In Despatches for his heroism. For some unknown reason he was not considered for a Victoria Cross immediately following the raid. At some point during the following months, his gallantry and that of Lt. Commander Arthur L. Harrison (who led the parties from the Vindictive onto the mole) were recognised. On the 23rd February 1919, Vice Admiral Keyes wrote a recommendation to the Admiralty for the award of the Victoria Cross to Bradford and Harrison. Of George he said:

> Though securing the ship was not part of his duties Lieut. Commander Bradford climbed up the derrick, which carried a large parapet anchor and was rigged out over the port side; during this climb the ship was surging up and down and the derrick crashing on the Mole; waiting his opportunity he jumped with the parapet anchor on to the Mole and placed it in position.

> Immediately after hooking on the parapet anchor, Lieut. Commander Bradford was riddled with bullets from machine guns and fell into the sea between the Mole and the ship. Attempts to recover his body failed.

> Lieut. Commander Bradford's action was one of absolute self-sacrifice; without a moment's hesitation he went to certain death, recognising that in such action lay the only possible chance of securing "Iris II" and enabling her storming parties to land.

The citation for the Victoria Cross was published in the *London Gazette* on the 17th March 1919. The medal was presented to George's mother at Buckingham Palace on the 3rd April. It was her third visit to the Palace to receive medals awarded to her dead sons. The King was heard to remark, 'What, you again!'

Thomas Bradford was now the only surviving brother and still serving in Ireland. He wrote to his mother on the 27th April 1919:

> My dear Mother,
>
> I saw Lieut. Henderson at the Admiralty today and he gave me the following account:
>
> The Iris was run against the Quay and George jumped from her deck upon the Quay and lay there for about three minutes shouting for those on deck to throw the grappling iron, which they did and he made it fast. He thinks he must have been hit by a machine gun bullet as he fell into the water. They threw him a line, which he grasped but he thinks George died at that moment because his grip on the rope relaxed and he sank, dying after he knew he had done his work and without pain, a most gallant deed.
>
> We have just got to bear up and look at it from George's point of view, a glorious career nobly and for him happily ended.
>
> I hope Amy and you are well and also Aunt Fanny and Uncle Robert.
>
> Your affec. son,
>
> Tommie.

This account seems to indicate that Lt. Henderson was an eyewitness to the event. Though it differs in some respect from the account given earlier, the essentials are the same. Letters of commiseration arrived at the mother's home, now in Kent. Amongst these was one from Admiral Viscount Jellicoe:

> I remember your son so well, and admired his character as well as his great personal ability. The Service and the Country have indeed lost in him one who could ill be spared. He died, as one would have expected him to die, under circumstances of the greatest gallantry and with supreme self-sacrifice. For one who is very proud to have had so gallant an officer and so perfect a gentleman under his command.

Capt. Fullerton commanded Bradford's ship. He too wrote to George's mother:

> I can truly say a more honourable, straight and gallant English gentleman never lived, and his loss is not only great to us, his shipmates, but also a loss to the country and the world. He was loved by all...I have no doubt you know that your son was picked from the whole of the 2nd Battle Squadron to command our men.

The Chaplain of the Orion also sent commiserations:

> He was so magnificent, so firm and patient and kind that we all, both officers and men, looked to him for guidance and advice...The news of his death in the amazingly gallant attack on the German forts came as a great sorrow to every man in the ship. I was besieged wherever I went that morning with inquiries whether the report of his death was true... The Boys, who were George's special care in the Orion, naturally loved him. 'He always had a smile for us,' one of them told me the other day, a description of himself which would have amused George, who used laughingly to say he was growing too serious.
>
> For myself, I like to think of George as he knelt among the men at communion; he would be there every alternate Sunday, and I am sure that his presence, because of his whole life, was a source of encouragement to many weaker ones, as it was a continual inspiration to myself.

Vice Admiral Keyes, who planned and commanded the assault, wrote to Mrs. Bradford on the 14th March 1919:

> You may hear before my letter reaches you that your very gallant son George has been awarded the posthumous Victoria Cross which he so heroically earned on his birthday.
>
> I knew he would eventually get it, because although many actions were performed on that night by officers and men who survived, and by others who gave their lives, amongst the latter your son's act of glorious self-sacrifice stood out, I thought alone. It will be a very great satisfaction to many in the Service, who loved him and knew his worth, that he should have been selected with one other to represent the gallant throng who did not survive.
>
> I know how deeply you have suffered in this war, but to have been the Mother of such splendid sons must have some consolation to you. In all Sympathy.

Three days later, Mrs. Bradford received the following telegram from the Admiralty:

Have much pleasure in informing you that the King has approved the posthumous award of the Victoria Cross to you son the late Cdr. George Bradford.

Capt. Alfred F.B. Carpenter, who commanded the Vindictive on the Zeebrugge Raid and was also awarded the Victoria Cross, wrote to Mrs. Bradford in April 1921. He had just completed his book on the raid, *The Blocking of Zeebrugge*, and in his letter he asked her if she had a photograph of her son that he could reproduce:

As a result of giving many lectures on the raid I have been implored to put the whole story in book form so that such heroic deeds as that of your son may be permanently recorded. I found it extremely difficult to do him justice in the book because my enthusiasm concerning his gallantry cannot be measured by mere words. His death was a terrible blow to us all, we feel, however, that we should be better men for having known him. He was a great gentleman and loved by all with whom he was associated and his name will go down in history and act as a spur to the coming generations whose emotions will bestirred deeply whenever his splendid deed is mentioned.

If George's deed no longer stirs generations who are not likely to have heard of him, his courage is of the stuff echoed down the centuries whenever brave men have had to place themselves at the forefront in violent action in defence of their country.

George was the third of the Bradford brothers to be killed in action, all within a year of savage warfare. The effect this had on their mother cannot be measured. Her hard and often harsh life with her husband, combined with these terrible blows, caused an eccentricity of behaviour that may have enabled her to cope with her loss. After the war she moved back to her native Kent and lived with her two sisters for the rest of her life at Ravenlea Road, Folkestone, in a house she renamed Milbanke. She often made short visits to the North East to see Thomas, her surviving son.

She became a member of the Holy Trinity and Christ Church and a life member of the Association of Men of Kent and Kentish Men. At every Remembrance Day ceremony in Folkestone after World War I, she appeared wearing the two Victoria Crosses and the Military Cross her sons had earned. When she grew too old to do this Amy took her place. Mrs. Bradford died on Sunday, 7 January 1951, aged 91 years.

Her Grandson George wrote:

[She] moved back to her beloved Kent and, I think, in spite of the losses of her sons, she came to know a sort of happiness, even if it was achieved by shutting off chapters of the past.

Chapter 10

THE POST-WAR YEARS

Shortly after the end of the war, Thomas Bradford left the army. He acquired a farm under Yeavering Bell, Northumberland, and lived there for some time with his wife, Rebe. In 1919, they had a son, whom they baptized with the names of the brothers who were killed in the war: George James Roland Bradford. Young George grew up to be a complete contrast to his father. Where Thomas was tough and athletic, George was interested almost exclusively in the arts and music, and made a career in acting. George wrote of his father:

> In middle age, my father was a rigid sort of man, whatever mellowness he acquired came with age…Gallant soldier, games player, fisherman and a good shot, he was everything I would never be. Both he and my mother may not have approved or understood, yet for the most part, they were tolerant and helpful.

Though George chose a life in the theatre, when the time came he did take up the family legacy and served in World War Two. While his forebears fought in the front lines, however, George served as an entertainments officer with his regiment.

In time, Rebe became homesick for Durham and persuaded Thomas to return to her family home in Acorn Close, Sacriston, where he found work in agriculture. George wrote:

> Thanks to his father-in-law he was now looking after colliery farms [owned by Col. Blackett], assessing compensation for the crop damage frequently caused by the giant burrowing beneath them.

In keeping with his upbringing, Thomas took an interest in local politics and affairs. In October, 1922, he stood for Parliament as a Conservative candidate for the Seaham Division of Durham, but lost the seat to the Labour candidate, Sidney Webb. Again, in the general election of December 1923, Thomas stood as the Conservative candidate for the Durham Division where he suffered defeat by 3,200 votes. The same year, he and his family moved to Aden Cottage, just on the outskirts of Durham City.

Electoral setbacks did not deter Thomas from an active public life. In 1939, he was knighted for his public services. In 1942, he served as High Sheriff for the County of Durham, and was a magistrate from 1939 to 1961. His titles and interests did not end there. He was Deputy Lieutenant to Lord Londonderry, Honorary Treasurer of Durham University, and held directorships in the North East Housing Association, Charlaw and Sacriston Collieries and a number of other companies. Later he became a surveyor with the National Coal Board. In addition, he continued his military interests, County Cadet Commander and Honorary Colonel of the

17th Battalion, Parachute Regiment (9th Battalion The Durham Light Infantry). He worked long and hard for the Durham Light Infantry Regimental Association.

Thomas's personality is best described by his nephew (Amy's son) Jonathan Cremer, who wrote:

> As a young boy growing up, I clearly remember that when I met "Uncle Tommie" I had to be prepared to receive and extremely firm handshake and that it would be accompanied by the words, 'Now look me straight in the eyeball!'...If I failed to do that, he would insist upon our starting the handshaking all over again!

Amy Bradford and Harry Leslie Creamer, after their wedding.

While Thomas kept up the Bradford presence in the North East, sister Amy had married Harry Leslie Creamer and moved to his home town in Kent. She had four children, all of whom she gave the third name 'Bradford': David George Bradford Creamer, Roland Paul Bradford Creamer, Jonathan Leslie and Waveney Joanna Rachel Bradford Creamer. Amy and her family made frequent trips to the North East. Jonathan recalled what visiting 'Uncle Tommie' was like:

> My experiences of Tommie were that he was a kindly and quite jovial man. He was somewhat eccentric in many ways and was an absolute stickler for

'Uncle Tommy' with Rufus, c. 1960.

detail but no trace of brutality ever shone through. It is certainly true that I was in awe (respect) of him as I grew up. But that was only because he was so totally unlike any other man I had ever met...

Tommie was extremely generous. Several times he gave me considerable gifts (for your 'privy purse' he would say) because he said he wanted to see us enjoying his gifts rather than leave money to us after he was dead.

Aden Cottage, Whitesmocks, Durham, c. mid-1950s.

The saying 'Le Chevalier sans peu et sans reproche' was obviously a quotation of some significance within Tommie's experience because I remember his enjoining me to aspire to that moral value more than once (in writing) whilst I was growing up – originally I believe used in the writings of one Pierre Bayard back in the 16th Century or perhaps earlier than that...My trips to his home at Aden Cottage I always regard as being the highest points of my childhood

When World War Two broke out, the Bradford family must have braced itself, particularly Thomas and Amy. Having witnessed so much, they knew all too well the implications of war. Despite all they had lost, however, the family did not harbour grudges. Jonathan Cremer wrote:

An interesting thing that I have always been most aware of...is that in my entire life I have never even detected even the slightest hint of bitterness towards the German race...When the Second World War began there was no sign in Tommie or my mother Amy Isabelle that, 'Here we are again dealing with this dreadful race of people that cut down our brothers in the prime of their lives'. Such feelings appeared to be totally absent.

Thomas's wife Rebe Bradford died in 1945. Unfortunately, there are no records of any illness or cause of death. Some time afterwards, he married Kitty Percy, the widow of Brig. Jos Percy who had commanded the 9th Battalion DLI in France and the Western Desert during WWII. He also commanded 151 Brigade at the Battle of Alamein in October/November 1942. Kitty was already the mother of two sons and a daughter. George junior wrote:

At the time it may have seemed to be bringing advantage to both of them, to her a secure future and a home for her family. To him, someone familiar to cope with the day-to-day things and pleasant children around him, the boys interested in suitable, boyish things, just as he had once been.

Thomas Bradford lived at Aden Cottage for the rest of his life, and died peacefully there on the 30th December, 1966, aged 80 years.

Loved by his family, Thomas was also held in great affection by others. On the occasion of his death a friend wrote:

> Tommy Bradford achieved an outstanding position in the County of Durham. He was loved and respected by all who had the interests of the County at heart, whatever their persuasions, politics and jobs might be. And all came to him for counsel and advice. His great sense of humour and his endless fund of improbable stories, made all such approaches a rewarding experience, and served to sugar many pills.
>
> He had an abiding interest in everything to do with the Regiment, and we are much in his debt for his able Chairmanship of the Regimental Fund for the difficult years following the end of the war.
>
> He had a great love of country, and was a great sportsman. Excellent at cricket and ball games in his younger days and devoted to his gun and salmon rod in later years…A great character who will be sorely missed.

The last of the Bradford brothers, Thomas had a full and active life. A source of strength and dedicated to the service of others, he is a glimpse of what his brothers might have accomplished had their lives not been cut so tragically short.

Chapter 11

THE BRADFORD LEGACY

The North East of England has many tributes to the Bradfords. From monuments to windows, their memory echoes through the landscapes of County Durham. One of the largest memorials is the Bradford Entrance at the Darlington Memorial Hospital. Dedicated most specifically to Roland, a subscription list was opened in the early 1920s to build a monument, and its organising committee had Gen. Sir William Robertson, GCB, as its president, H. Pike Pease MP as honorary treasurer and Sir Charles Starmer as honorary secretary. Donations ranging from £105 from the wealthiest benefactors to mere pennies from the poorest were received. Prominent contributors included the Earl of Durham, the Pease family, proprietors of the *Northern Echo* and *North Star* newspapers, the Earl of Harewood, Lord Northbourne, Lord Glanely and many other local and national notables. The total sum of £3,000 was donated to build the hospital entrance, whose entry is engraved with the names of all the Darlington men killed in the Great War of 1914–1918. Prince George himself opened the hospital on 5th May 1933, and prominent among the notables was Thomas Bradford.

In addition to the hospital, a monument in memory of Roland was erected at St. Cuthbert's Church, Darlington. Unveiled by Herbert Hensley Henson DD, Lord Bishop of Durham on 19th July 1925, the dedication is located on the east wall of the north transept. The service included an appreciation written by John Buchan:

In the long roll of young dead, Roland Bradford is in some ways the most conspicuous figure. In three years of war he had made a great career, and he fell at the age of 25, the youngest general in the British Army. His family, which contains both Durham and Kentish strains, had a battle record that few can equal.

Another tribute is a memorial tablet to all the brothers above the door to the vestry in the Holy Trinity Church, Darlington, and a window that was placed in St. Paul's Church, Witton Park, in July 1989. A further memorial to the brothers was dedicated in the Queen Elizabeth Grammar School, Darlington, which they had attended as children (now called the Queen Elizabeth Sixth Form College).

In addition to memorial in stone and glass, Roland's actions in particular have found their way into many history books. In his book *Rommel* Brig. Desmond Young states:

In all armies there is a small minority of professional soldiers (and a few amateurs) who find in war the one occupation to which they are perfectly adapted. Year by year in the "In Memoriam" column of *The Times*, my eye catches the name of Brigadier-General "Boy" Bradford, V.C., M.C., killed in the Cambrai battle in 1917 at the age of

24 [actually 25], and I remember riding over, unduly conspicuous, I felt, on a white horse, to his brigade head-quarters in front of Bourlon Wood and thinking, as I talked to him, that here was someone at last who knew his trade and was equal to any demands that war might make.

As well as history, there is at least one fiction author who took inspiration from Roland's story. In the series *A Chronicle of Ancient Sunlight* by Henry Williamson, one volume entitled *Love and the Loveless* is set in 1917. A chapter of this book is headed 'The Boy General'. As Keith Simpson of the Department of War Studies, Sandhurst Royal Military Academy, attested in a letter dated 4th October 1973, the 'Boy General' was Roland Boys Bradford.

Not surprisingly, most of the way the Bradfords are remembered is connected to the military. Thomas Bradford officially opened Darlington's new Territorial Army Centre on Neasham Road on 5th October 1963. In fitting dedication, the Centre is named 'The Bradford Armoury'. Likewise, the Durham Light Infantry Museum and Durham Art Gallery houses Roland's Victoria Cross and James's Military Cross, and has permanent displays to the family including Roland's jacket. The cards that Roland printed for his men still circulate, and when he commissioned the image for 'Abide with Me', the artist painted a copy. This oil painting is now held in the permanent collection of the Shipley Gallery, Gateshead. 'Abide with Me' was the anthem of the 9th Battalion DLI until it was eventually absorbed into the Territorial Army in 1967. Whenever veterans of the regiment gather, this hymn is sung to this day, and the words echo of strength, faith and courage:

I fear no foe with thee at hand to bless;
Ills have no weight, and tears no bitterness.
Where is death's sting? Where grave thy victory?
I triumph still, if thou abide with me.

Hold thou thy cross before my closing eyes;
Shine through the gloom, and point me to the skies:
Heaven's morning breaks, and the earth's vain shadows flee;
In life, in death, O Lord, abide with me.

A question hangs over the Bradford brothers. Had George, James and Roland lived, what would they have become? As the youngest Brigadier General in the Army, what would have happened to Roland? He particularly invites comparison with other leaders of World War One who survived. Field Marshall Montgomery, who commanded the British Armies to victory in Northwest Europe during World War Two and won at Alamein, was a lowly Staff Captain when Roland died in 1917. Field Marshal Alexander, Supreme Commander of the Allied forces in Italy until the end of World War Two, was a mere Lieutenant Colonel commanding the 2nd Battalion Irish Guards. Might they have had to step aside for Field Marshal Bradford? We will never know, but Roland and his brothers have become beacons of courage and duty, and it is hoped that they will not be completely forgotten. They join a long line of heroes who have carved their names into the history of

Britain, and certainly they earned their name of the 'Fighting Bradfords'. As the epigraph of the family book states, 'No one died with more glory, yet many died and there was much glory'.

Acknowledgements

This book is the final product of many years of research and could not have been written without the assistance and support of a number of people.

The encouragement and support of Jonathan Cremer and his family is gratefully acknowledged. Jonathan gave me permission to use information from the Bradford website about his uncles, the Bradford brothers, and the family background and provided many of the family photographs which appear in the book (www.geocities.com/bradcrem/bradford). My first contact with the family was with George James Roland Bradford, the late son of Sir Thomas Bradford, and I am extremely grateful for his letters and unpublished autobiography, which he made available to me, and the wealth of material he provided on the family background.

Thanks are also due to Stephen Shannon, Manager of The Durham Light Infantry Museum, for his patience when dealing with my many requests for information and material from the Regimental Archives now held at the Durham County Record Office, County Hall, Durham. Mr George Fraser, also of the museum, readily responded to my requests for information from his records. A mention is also due to George Harwood, whose support and research has been appreciated. I am also grateful for the assistance of Ms. Jill Parkes, assistant archivist, and the staff of the County Archivist's Search Room. My thanks also for permission given from the Sound Archives Department of the Imperial War Museum to quote from the interview with Lt. Col. Rodney Gee MC.

I wish to acknowledge the role of Carol Smith and her staff of County Durham Books for making the publication of this book possible and, particularly, to Peg Osterman whose task as editor cannot have been an easy one and who carried it out with much patience and skill.

As ever, I have always had the support of my wife Audrey and my family and I thank them for their encouragement, understanding and patience' particularly my daughter Margaret who typed much of the final script and guided me through the intricacies of word processing, and my son Michael, whose interest in World War One surpasses my own.

Bibliography

Anonymous, *Brigadier-General R.B. Bradford VC, MC and His Brothers*, undated publication produced in a limited printing of 300 after World War One for the Bradford family (Ray Westlake, Military Books, Newport, South Wales).

Major Crouch DCM, *The Crouch Papers*, Durham County Record Office.

Durham County Archivists, *The Bradford Papers*.

History of the Northumberland Yeomanry 1819–1923 (Regimental Museum, Newcastle upon Tyne).

Brian Hunt, *100 Years of Durham County Cricket Club* (1983).

Commander John Irvine, *The Smokescreen of Jutland* (Wm. Kimber, 1966).

Admiral Viscount Jellicoe, *The Grand Fleet 1914–16* (Cassell, 1919).

Lt.Col. W.D. Lowe DSO, MC, *The 18th Battalion Durham Light Infantry* (Oxford University Press, 1920).

Harry Moses, *The Faithful Sixth: A History of the 6th Battalion Durham Light Infantry* (County Durham Books, 1995).

Harry Moses, *The Gateshead Gurkhas: A History of the 9th Battalion Durham Light Infantry 1859–1967* (County Durham Books, 2001).

Barrie Pitt, Zeebrugge, *St. George's Day 1918* (Cassell, 1958).

Capt. Alfred E.B. Carpenter VC, RN, *The Blocking of Zeebrugge* (Herbert Jenkins Ltd, 1922).

Lyn MacDonald, *1914* (Penguin Books, 1987).

Official Histories of the Great War: France & Belgium: 1914–1918 (HMSO).

Col. W.D.B. Thompson, *The Thompson Papers*, Durham County Archivists.

Major E.H. Veitch MC, *The Eighth Battalion The Durham Light Infantry 1793–1926* (J.H. Veitch & Son Ltd)

War Diaries of the 2nd, 7th, and 9th Battalions Durham Light Infantry 1914–1918, Durham County Archivists.

Everard Wyrell, *The History of the 50th Division* (Lund, Humphreys & Co. Ltd,

1939).

Everard Wyrell, *The History of the 62nd (West Riding) Division 1914–1919*, Vol.1 (Bodley Head Ltd).

Brigadier Desmond Young, *Rommel* (1950).